Praise for *Spark Change*

"In a world where bold thinking shapes our destiny, *Spark Change: 25 Tools for Strategic Thinking in For-Purpose Organisations* stands out as an indispensable guide. George's insights transcend the ordinary, urging us to elevate our decision-making process. After all, it's these decisions that separate the merely good from the truly great.

As a purpose-led executive, I found George's book to be a compass in uncharted waters. It not only challenged my biases but also provided practical strategies to navigate the complex landscape of organisational challenges and opportunities. From boardrooms to everyday choices, *Spark Change* empowers us to think beyond the obvious, igniting a transformative journey.

If you're ready to embrace bigger ideas and drive meaningful change, this book is your compass. Let it spark the fire within you."

GREG MULLER, Chair & Co-Founder, The United Project Foundation

"I think this is a great resource for new and establishing leaders in any organisation. It is also important reading for people already in leadership. I've seen George's work in action and the practical insights, resources and training suggested in this book are a really generous synthesis of so much of his experience. In any project I've worked on with him he has supported his clients to extend their thinking. That approach is reflected in this book, which focuses our attention on what we should be thinking when we're doing the *strategic* thinking—it's a fabulous tool for reminding you *how* to get to a good outcome."

TOM DALTON, Chief Executive Officer, Neami National

"In *Spark Change*, George Liacos masterfully distils decades of unparalleled experience at the forefront of for-purpose leadership and strategy. It offers a series of powerful, practical reflections and strategies for those committed to social impact. George's deep understanding of the challenges and opportunities facing for-purpose organisations today is evident on every page, making this book an invaluable toolkit for leaders and teams eager to refine their decision-making and amplify their impact. A must-read for the changemaker in all of us."

IAN PATTERSON, Chief Executive Officer, Humaniti

SPARK
CHANGE

SPARK

CHANGE

25 Tools for Strategic Thinking
in For-Purpose Organisations

GEORGE LIACOS

Published by Grammar Factory Publishing,
an imprint of MacMillan Company Limited.

Grammar Factory Publishing
MacMillan Company Limited
25 Telegram Mews, 39th Floor, Suite 3906
Toronto, Ontario, Canada
M5V 3Z1

www.grammarfactory.com

Liacos, George
Spark Change: 25 Tools for Strategic Thinking in
For-Purpose Organisations / George Liacos.

Paperback ISBN 978-1-998756-63-6
Hardcover ISBN 978-1-998756-65-0
eBook ISBN 978-1-998756-64-3

1. BUS019000 BUSINESS & ECONOMICS / Decision-Making
& Problem Solving. 2. BUS063000 BUSINESS & ECONOMICS /
Strategic Planning. 3. BUS074030 BUSINESS & ECONOMICS /
Nonprofit Organizations & Charities / Management & Leadership.

PRODUCTION CREDITS
Cover design by Designerbility
Interior layout design by Setareh Ashrafologhalai
Book production and editorial services by Grammar Factory Publishing

Grammar Factory's Carbon Neutral Publishing Commitment
Grammar Factory Publishing is proud to be neutralising the carbon
footprint of all printed copies of its authors' books printed by or ordered
directly through Grammar Factory or its affiliated companies through
the purchase of Gold Standard-Certified International Offsets.

A QUESTION that I love ...

We are told that our universe started with the Big Bang and has been expanding in the shape of a rugby football ever since.

We are told that if we travel far enough in a straight line out into this football-shaped universe, in any given direction, that we will eventually end up back at our starting point.

So we can't escape the football ...

But outside the football, what is our football universe expanding into?

... and what's outside that?

... and how do we get there?

Evil Kala: We're going to empty your memory as we might empty your pockets, Doctor.

Dr Hans Zarkov: Don't empty my mind! Please, I beg you! My mind is all I have! I've spent my whole life trying to fill it!

Flash Gordon, 1980

Let's fill up minds!

CONTENTS

AUTHOR'S NOTE

I'VE LEARNED a lot in writing this book. It's the fifth attempt, with the first being well before the pandemic.

That first attempt saw me exploring leadership and culture during the implementation of strategy in the social sector, and its shape and nub are patiently waiting for me to circle back. But I suspect the delay is more about me finding an interesting, juicy and non-academic way to share this often dry material!

As you will see, this book is far removed from that first topic on leadership. I guess my thinking has travelled down the causal links to try to unpack the first issue facing leaders in this sector, and I've landed on strategic thinking.

So with this said, there are three things I want to share with you before we start . . .

First: This book is meant to be a quick reference guide. To make this work for you I have used two devices: the Spark Navigator and loads of lists. I just want to shout out to my editor, Carolyn Jackson, about the Spark Navigator. I had feedback from my beta readers that we needed a way to help you quickly find the best Spark to fit your current problem. I had a go at this and was about to give up when Carolyn leapt boldly into the fray and kicked me into action by providing the framework you see in this book—thanks Carolyn and we hope it speeds you on your journey!

As for lists, I know that when I want to cut to the chase I like a good list. So that is what we have done here. We have dialled back on the prose and amplified the lists so you can get to the meat super fast.

Second: This book is drawn heavily from the work we do at Spark Strategy, but much of that work is confidential. In order to maintain this confidentiality while extracting key lessons, I have used two devices: fun little sci-fi stories to introduce each topic, and case studies to show how things work in the real world. The sci-fi stories are pure fiction, and for the case studies, I have changed the names of most of the organisations and sectors, and have sometimes blended the stories as well.

Third: Spark #8 is called Collaborative Intelligence, and is all about the blending of human and artificial intelligence to develop deeper insights or crunch large volumes of information. I have promised to let my readers know when I use AI in my work, so I have to tell you that I have used it to produce this book. I find it a terrific tool for specific tasks, such as research. I also use it to ask questions in a recursive way to help me organise my own thinking or move past blank page fever. It has also helped me with the sci-fi stories by coming up with goofy plotlines or names for planets and aliens. We couldn't find these names or plotlines in our research, but if you are a sci-fi author and one of your names appears here, both apologies and heartfelt thanks for helping us build sector capability for more and better social change.

INTRODUCTION

JENNIFER IS the seasoned leader of a busy for-purpose workplace. There is always so much work to do, rarely enough resources to do it, and it's so very hard to find enough of the right people to do this important work.

Every day, Jennifer faces problems that keep re-occurring no matter how many operational band-aids she sticks on. There is also a steady stream of opportunities that would make things so much easier and the services they deliver so much better, but she can't quite get to them ... even though she knows the difference it would make if she could.

Jennifer knows the block to getting to these bigger issues and opportunities is not just her lack of time; it's in her team's headspace, in the way they think and act. Jennifer loves her team; for all their faults and fails, they are wonderful humans trying to do better and be better. All too busy and trying hard with not enough resources. But sometimes she wishes they would lift their chins and look up. Just a little. She wishes that her team could see the bigger issues, better long-run solutions and, maybe even more, the bigger opportunities. Jennifer wishes they could stop getting swamped by the daily work long enough to just think. That they could get on the front foot and not only start solving the root causes of their daily pains, but imagining and innovating a whole new future for their workplace.

'Why can I see these solutions and these possibilities, but not my team?' Jennifer asks herself.

'They're just too busy,' she answers, feeling protective.

And like many purpose-led leaders, Jennifer takes on the load.

'I'll just push that meeting back and maybe skip gym, just for today, so I can make the space to think about this a bit more,' . . . again.

As Jennifer pours herself a coffee, she wonders, 'How is it I can see these things, think this way?'

Jennifer has a trusted adviser, Maria, who is the owner of a digital media company they work with. They often grab a coffee and chat about work, impact and all that stuff. Jennifer asks Maria if she is experiencing the same thing.

'Totally. I've done my MBA and I scroll, probably too much,' says Maria, and then reflection washes across her face.

'I've realised that the MBA was great in showing me how to do strategic planning, but it's not the planning bit I had developed. I think experience has taught me how to see problems in a broader light and have different mental and practical tools to attack those problems. I think they call this "strategic thinking" and I wish I could magically download this experience to my team's brains,' Maria says.

'I know my team would be more aligned and we would be making serious leaps towards our goals if we could line up on this,' she adds.

'Oh, I know,' Jennifer agrees. 'I can already see what things could be like if we could all be able to think this way and line up together. I guess it's part of what I've dreamed about when I think about having a high-performance leadership team.'

The problem

Leaders are being asked to plan strategically without knowing how to think strategically.

Hang on a minute, I can hear you say. Aren't they the same thing? No, they're not, and please bear with me for a brief (ish) segue…

Strategic thinking and strategic planning are two phrases often bandied about in boardrooms, strategy workshops and all sorts of professional conversations. But let's get one thing crystal clear: these are not interchangeable terms.

Strategic thinking is the art of the possible, the potential and the long term. It's a mindset, an approach that enables you to think beyond the here and now—not just one or two steps ahead, but miles into the future. It's about outwitting, outmanoeuvring and outlasting your problems in a way that's innovative, adaptive and, above all, proactive. Think of it as an explorer's spirit, the compass that guides you through uncharted territory. It's about asking, 'What if?' and 'Why not?' It's where imagination meets acumen to form insight. This is the realm where visionaries or social sector game changers like Muhammad Yunus dwell. It's fluid, dynamic and expansive.

Strategic planning, on the other hand, is far more structured. It takes the myriad possibilities generated by strategic thinking and converts them into actionable, measurable plans. It's where you decide on the 'how', 'when' and 'who'.

The relationship between strategic thinking and planning is symbiotic. You can't have one without the other if you expect to make any meaningful progress. Think of it this way: strategic thinking is your business philosophy, while strategic planning is your business model. Like yin and yang, they complement and complete each other.

You turn to strategic thinking when you're looking to disrupt an existing sector, create a new service line or solve social problems in innovative ways. It allows for adaptability and is open to taking calculated risks. This is where you ask, 'What problem is society not solving, and how can we address it?'

Strategic planning kicks in when you've decided on the avenue you'll venture down. This is where you work out the complexities and allocate resources, whether that's time, money or workforce. It's also where risk management happens, providing a safety net for your ambitions.

Is one superior to the other? Not a chance. They're two sides of the same coin. Strategic thinking without strategic planning is like having a dream but no resolve to realise it. Conversely, planning without thinking is a rigid construct that's more likely to collapse than adapt when met with unexpected challenges.

So, back to the problem at hand. I said that leaders are being asked to **plan** strategically without knowing how to **think** strategically. This is like asking someone to run a marathon without training, or play basketball having only ever watched a game.

I would argue that the majority of nonprofit and for-purpose strategic plans I have seen reflect this. They lack the insights, ideas and rigour they could have, which leads to mis-spending scarce resources and limited impact. Heart-loads of goodwill, yet just spoonfuls of impact.

The world is changing fast. Yep, that's a cliche, but it's true.

Leaders need to be able to anticipate and understand these impending changes and then adapt at light speed. To see, understand and adapt, they need to have a well-developed strategic thinking muscle ... and the vast majority of leaders I have worked with don't.

So, they shuffle off to study MBAs in their flagship strategy courses, they hit the Kindle store looking for books on strategy, or they Google themselves into a rabbit warren and end up with brains full but not yet thinking strategically.

The current education and literature is focused on strategic *planning*, and the methods, processes and tools to do this. But what nobody tells you is that strategic planning stands on the shoulders of strategic *thinking* and no method, process or tool out there can replace how you think. Further, there is limited material or practical guidance on how to develop your strategic thinking muscle. As a colleague once said, 'It's 100 per cent on the job, and wouldn't it be great if it wasn't?!'

Then there's a confidence problem. Some leaders believe that they 'just can't think this way'. Some are newer executives who haven't developed their strategic thinking muscle. All of them are part of teams who can only move as fast as the slowest member.

There is a simple reason for this. Developing your strategic thinking muscle requires learning from many diverse and powerful disciplines. And it's hard to pull all these disciplines together into a cohesive and practical guide.

But I believe that people everywhere *can* 'think this way'. It's like singing. With the right training and practise, anyone can be taught to sing. It's the same with the strategic thinking muscle; it takes training and practise.

Training this muscle is not something that happens hunched over books or in the confines of a course. That's just one part of the muscle-building routine. The strategic muscle fibres are built through learning ways of thinking and having access to tools and techniques. The muscle mass comes through repeated use in live situations. I have also found that this mass is built faster when done as part of a team. This is because we each bring a unique perspective that influences and accelerates individual learning. It shares our strategic thinking muscle.

But where to start? There is so much literature out there on strategy. So much to wade through. Much of it on strategic planning and very little of it on how to think in a live situation. And different problems and opportunities need different strategic thinking muscles. You might be wondering, 'How do I work out where to go and what to tap into for any given situation? And even if I get it right, how do I get my team on the same page and building the muscles they need to make us all power forward?'

The solution

Before we play in the sandpit of strategic planning, we need a way to both help new leaders quickly build this muscle mass, and keep more experienced leaders toned up. A way that gives us practical techniques and tools to practise and train with, both alone and together. Something that helps us to anticipate and understand strategic opportunities and threats as well as the live problems we face today.

Despite popular belief that strategists sit around in deep hoods, chanting some secret and sacred rite that no one else can possibly hope to learn, strategic thinking is inherently available to everyone. What we need, in fact, is a way for anyone to build their strategic thinking muscle, both as individual players and as a team—so we can all play.

Given how busy we are, we also need a fast and easy way to get what we need when we need it. We need the thinking equivalent of a twenty-four-hour Kieser gym. If you're not familiar with Kieser, it's a gym staffed by physiotherapists and exercise physiologists, and has a bunch of very precise weight machines that strap you in and lock you down so that you can only exercise a particular muscle. Great for rehab—I should know! Train only what we need, when we need it.

This is why I have dug into my decades of experience and identified seventy-five ways to think strategically. The first twenty-five are here for you to explore. Why these twenty-five? Well, two reasons really—the first is that I think they are the most useful or more frequently accessed. In fact, the first ten or so are probably the most useful and well used of all. Second, I needed to get the word count down and cutting seventy-five to twenty-five was a great way to do this!

These 'Sparks' describe ways of thinking strategically to help you anticipate and adapt so that you can survive and thrive. Each Spark is a discrete practice that presents an explanation, creates language and provides techniques to build your strategic thinking muscle. Each Spark is also crammed with quotes, case studies and hundreds of references and links to take the Google-mania out of learning. Purpose built for purposeful leaders.

This book helps build the strategic thinking muscle for leaders and their teams—together and individually. By using this book, you and your team will think more strategically and develop better strategy, which will lead to more and better impact.

How to use this book

If you have this book in your hand, you are probably someone who has been told to 'think strategically' or who really wishes your team could do more so. You are probably a leader or soon will be. You may be on a Board or two.

While I make no secret that I am trying to build capability and capacity in the nonprofit sector, I have written this book with equal care for government and corporate humans as well. My goal is that you can learn about a strategic thinking technique with your team or on your own, and then have a go at trying to apply the learning to a strategic issue you face.

I can imagine a leader (or a Chair) buying a box of these books and giving them to their team. Then I imagine the team getting together around a problem or opportunity, choosing one Spark (or more), and trying to address their issue through the lens of that Spark. In doing so, they build their individual and combined strategic thinking muscle.

I can also imagine someone picking one Spark a week and proactively finding a work problem to apply it to. Or, conversely, when they encounter a problem flicking through the Sparks to try one on for size or dropping down to the references to find a solution.

I wanted to write a book for you that is informative, easy to read and practical. So practical you can apply what you read in each chapter immediately. To that end, the content is presented in bite-sized chunks, and each strategic Spark is laid out across just a few pages in exactly the same way to help you understand, learn and practise the Spark. The structure looks like this:

1   Introduction by way of a sci-fi story—because I am a nerd (and I hope you get as much joy in reading them as I did in writing them)

2   When to use this Spark

3   How to use this Spark

4   Outcomes of using this Spark

5   Dangers to beware of

6   Muscle-building tools and techniques

7   A case study from the for-purpose sector

8   Resources and references

I know not everyone is into space and sci-fi, so if that's not your bag feel free to skip the section in each Spark that has the little rocket icon beside it.

As mentioned in my Author's Note, I have also included a 'Spark Navigator', a matrix that will help you zoom in on the right Spark or Sparks to solve particular problems.

In developing the content of this book, I've also created a variety of related materials that will help you expand your understanding of the Sparks and support the development of your strategic thinking skills or those of your team. To access these bonus materials, please visit www.sparkstrategy.com.au/bookbonus/

By now you might be wondering why I wrote this book. And what qualifies me to write it. So, let's go on a little journey...

Who am I?

I'm George Liacos and I've been a strategist for nearly three decades. For the last fifteen years I've focused on the for-purpose, not-for-profit and government sectors. I've worked with over 600 organisations, helping their leaders, teams and Boards to develop their strategic plans and, more importantly, their strategic thinking muscle.

About twenty-five years ago I founded the company now known as Spark Strategy, and fifteen years ago I pivoted towards the social sector. Today Spark Strategy is the leading specialist strategic advisory firm for the for-purpose sector. This gives me terrific joy, as literally every day I get to work with beautiful humans striving to change the world for others.

Alongside my advisory work, I have been delivering keynotes, webinars, masterclasses and writing on strategy, purpose and strategic thinking for longer than I care to remember. I really do like sharing what I'm seeing and learning because I believe that together, we can do better. Why do I do these things? Because I believe that all our social problems are solvable, and that as a community we are just choosing not to solve them.

My own purpose is to help people make different decisions; decisions that lead to more and better impact. I do this by helping them to find and build their strategic thinking muscle for themselves, their workplaces and their world.

I am more than 1,000 strategy workshops in now, and at almost every one I have found myself in a kind of trance and channelling or saying a phrase that just pulled everything and everyone together. (My team always scrambles to catch me in this moment. 'Say that again!!!!') What happens in these moments is that my mind is working on the problem in a multitude of ways all at the same time, and it is this ability that sits in front of good strategic planning. In the beginning, I didn't have an external frame or method for this channelling—I felt like I was making it up—but I came to learn that nothing was further from the truth. I was naturally and cohesively thinking strategically.

So, with this little bit of context about me and my journey, I humbly offer you this guide to developing your strategic thinking muscle. This is a book full of learnings, experiences, references and hope. All presented as a smorgasbord of morsels that you can and should nibble at.

Come on. Jump in!

THE SPARK
NAVIGATOR

THIS BOOK is designed to be picked up and dipped into at any point—it's not a narrative! But where to start? Of course, you can sit down and read the book from start to finish in one go if you like, but more often than not you'll have a particular issue you want to address, and need to know which Spark or Sparks will be most useful. This is where the following navigator comes in. Just look across to the top of the matrix to find which category your current issue belongs in, then run your finger down to find the ticks that indicate which Spark/s to try out.

	NAVIGATING CHANGE	RESOURCE MANAGEMENT	STAKEHOLDER ENGAGEMENT	STRATEGIC ALIGNMENT	INNOVATION & ADAPTABILITY	CULTURE & LEADERSHIP	FINANCIAL SUSTAINABILITY	SYSTEM REFORM	RISK MANAGEMENT
SPARK #1: PATTERN RECOGNITION	✓			✓	✓		✓	✓	
SPARK #2: CURIOSITY	✓			✓	✓		✓		
SPARK #3: GOLDEN THREAD			✓	✓				✓	
SPARK #4: KINDNESS			✓	✓		✓			
SPARK #5: TIMING – STRATEGY'S X FACTOR		✓			✓				✓
SPARK #6: HOLISTIC THINKING	✓				✓			✓	✓
SPARK #7: SPACE TO THINK	✓	✓		✓					✓
SPARK #8: COLLABORATIVE INTELLIGENCE H+AI	✓	✓			✓				
SPARK #9: TRIUNE BRAINS			✓	✓		✓			
SPARK #10: GETTING PAST YOURSELF		✓	✓			✓			
SPARK #11: VEIL OF RATIONALITY	✓				✓		✓		✓
SPARK #12: EMBRACING AMBIGUITY	✓		✓		✓		✓		
SPARK #13: CRITICAL THINKING		✓					✓	✓	✓

	NAVIGATING CHANGE	RESOURCE MANAGEMENT	STAKEHOLDER ENGAGEMENT	STRATEGIC ALIGNMENT	INNOVATION & ADAPTABILITY	CULTURE & LEADERSHIP	FINANCIAL SUSTAINABILITY	SYSTEM REFORM	RISK MANAGEMENT
SPARK #14: CONSTRUCTIVE SCEPTICISM	✓				✓		✓		✓
SPARK #15: BALANCING LONG AND SHORT TERM	✓			✓			✓		✓
SPARK #16: STRATEGIC AUTHENTICITY			✓	✓		✓			
SPARK #17: ASPIRATIONAL THINKING	✓			✓	✓		✓		
SPARK #18: STAKEHOLDER ENGAGEMENT		✓	✓					✓	
SPARK #19: ADAPTIVE CREATIVITY	✓	✓			✓				
SPARK #20: PURPOSEFUL THINKING			✓	✓		✓			
SPARK #21: ENVIRONMENTAL AWARENESS	✓				✓		✓	✓	✓
SPARK #22: PARTNERSHIPS		✓	✓					✓	
SPARK #23: SYSTEMS THINKING		✓					✓	✓	✓
SPARK #24: CONCEPTUAL BOUNDARY SPANNING	✓				✓			✓	✓
SPARK #25: SCENARIO THINKING	✓	✓			✓			✓	✓

In addition to the Spark Navigator table, we have also included a graphic to help you orient yourself. It includes nine categories:

1 Navigating Change (CH)
2 Resource Management (RE)
3 Stakeholder Engagement (ST)
4 Strategic Alignment (AL)
5 Innovation & Adaptability (IN)
6 Culture & Leadership (CL)
7 Financial Stability (FS)
8 System Reform (SR)
9 Risk Management (RI)

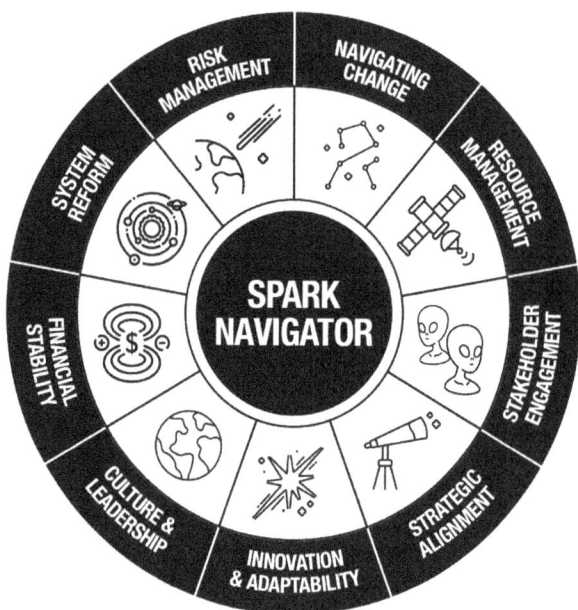

Within each Spark, you'll find a graphic that indicates which Spark Navigator category the Spark applies to. As well, under the 'When to use this Spark' heading, you'll find more detailed information about when to deploy it. Good luck!

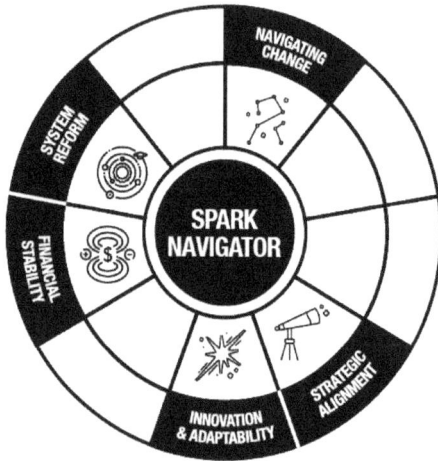

NAVIGATING CHANGE (CH)

STRATEGIC ALIGNMENT (AL)

INNOVATION & ADAPTABILITY (IN)

FINANCIAL STABILITY (FS)

SYSTEM REFORM (SR)

PATTERN
RECOGNITION

OKAY, LET'S get started with our first Spark!

Pattern recognition is a cornerstone of strategic thinking in any context. It is the intuitive ability to identify recurring themes or trends amid a sea of information. This cognitive skill allows us to see similarities or regularities in verbal or numerical information, images, or just about any kind of input we receive. This ability to identify patterns is pivotal in making informed, impactful decisions. Let me explain further by taking a little detour... to outer space.

Imagine you're overseeing a mission to terraform Mars. Forget a single rocket; you're sending an armada, packed with all sorts of technology, life-support systems and, of course, a human crew. You can't afford to rely solely on pre-calculated models because the universe doesn't play by fixed rules that we understand. You need help. You need the power of pattern recognition.

Let's say that one day you're meticulously scanning through data from previous space missions, both successful and failed. You notice that fuel consumption tends to spike when passing through certain cosmic conditions. Aha! That's a pattern. Or maybe you observe recurring minor failures in the life-support systems, but only when the spacecraft is closest to the Sun. Bang on, another pattern. Recognising these patterns allows you to adapt, in real-time. Maybe you alter the spacecraft's trajectory or tweak the life-support systems to withstand those solar flares better.

The genius of pattern recognition lies in its simplicity; it enables us to construct a coherent narrative from scattered fragments. It's a framework to map out the past, understand the present and, most critically, to anticipate the future. In the case of your mission to Mars, pattern recognition has provided you with a star-studded compass to help you identify potential problems in the uncharted regions of space.

It's easy to devolve pattern recognition into a data-centric scientific practice, but it's not just about tech algorithms and historical data. What I am saying is that in strategic thinking, pattern recognition is about blending data, lived experience and expert opinion in a dynamic way so that you can sense patterns.

Pattern recognition is an innate cognitive process, deeply rooted in the intricate workings of our neural pathways. It's an inherently human thing that we take for granted—it's the core of our intuition. Our brain, a marvel of evolutionary biology, is hardwired to discern patterns from the barrage of stimuli it encounters. Detecting recurring sequences in nature, like the rustle of leaves signalling a predator's approach or the visual pattern of a venomous snake, allowed for quicker, life-saving reactions.

In today's complex world, pattern recognition underpins our ability to make sense of vast amounts of information, be it in recognising market trends, deciphering social cues or, as I've often witnessed, crafting strategies that resonate with an organisation's core ethos.

🕐 When to use this Spark

Pattern recognition in strategic thinking is particularly effective in scenarios where historical data and trends are available. That is, stable, predictable environments where past performance is a reliable indicator of future outcomes. Unlike approaches that prioritise innovation or disruption, pattern recognition emphasises continuity and stability, making it particularly suitable for sectors or environments where consistency and predictability are valued.

Pattern recognition aligns well with technological advancements in data analysis and machine learning. When automation and AI are in the picture, pattern recognition can leverage these technologies to analyse large datasets, making it a modern and forward-looking approach.

How to use this Spark

I see concepts as pictures in my mind's eye. I rotate and move these mental images around, looking for patterns, links, gaps or new insights. A bit like the PC game *Assassin's Creed*. Or the iPad puzzle game *The Room*—where you see a set of shapes suspended in mid-air, use your mouse to alter your perspective on these shapes and move them around until they line up into a picture you can recognise.

I know that not everyone thinks like this, but my little example is meant to convey the sense that you access solid data, lived experience and expert opinion and assess them together—by moving and shifting your perspective and looking for a pattern.

So, how do you start thinking this way? I recommend following these steps:

1 Get your mind into 'intake mode'. Be ready to just take on as much information as you can cram in without feeling overwhelmed. For me it's a conscious activity to be calm, breathe and open my mind.

2 Gather and review the stimulus material (data, lived experience, expert opinion, contextual and environmental analysis).

3 Try to whiteboard the key concepts that come to you—freestyle a mind map.

4 Force yourself to think about other problems you have worked on and strategies you have developed

that might relate to this one and add them to the mind map. Do this by listing them out, thinking about each for a moment and then trying to find links or lessons learned.

5 Step back from the whiteboard, but don't try to read it. Your brain will take it in all by itself.

6 Pick up the pen and start capturing what comes to mind.

After some practise, these steps will happen so fast you won't have to think about them. No whiteboard and no mind map. You'll be like a seasoned physician who can probably diagnose your ailment before you reach the chair in their consulting room. This is heightened pattern recognition.

☑ The outcomes of using this Spark

Pattern recognition is a powerful tool in the realm of strategic thinking. Once you have mastered this skill, you will find that it yields practical, actionable outcomes. Let's look at some of those:

- **Enhanced predictive capabilities:** By analysing historical data and recognising trends, organisations can anticipate future challenges and opportunities more accurately. This foresight is critical in developing strategies that are not just reactive, but also proactive. It helps to optimise processes and systems, leveraging established patterns to enhance performance and productivity. This predictive capacity is invaluable in strategising for long-term outcomes and in anticipating market changes or societal shifts.

- **More informed decision-making:** In a landscape often cluttered with overwhelming amounts of data, the ability to discern relevant patterns enables leaders to cut through the noise and make informed decisions swiftly and confidently. It helps to identify market trends, customer behaviours and operational efficiencies, allowing for informed decision-making.

- **More objective decision-making:** Pattern recognition relies heavily on empirical data and observable trends, distinguishing it from more intuitive or theoretical approaches. This data-driven focus offers a more objective foundation for decision-making.

- **Better risk management:** Identifying and understanding patterns in past events or behaviours aids in pinpointing potential risks and vulnerabilities. This knowledge empowers organisations to devise strategies that mitigate risks effectively, safeguarding their operations and enhancing their resilience.

- **Optimised efficiency:** Recognising patterns in operational processes or stakeholder behaviours allows organisations to refine and streamline their methods, leading to increased efficiency and effectiveness.

Just as recognising a constellation amid a sea of stars can provide direction to a lost traveller, discerning patterns in the feedback, shifts and nuances of our communities equips us to navigate the intricate landscape of social change.

⚠ Dangers to beware of

Pattern recognition will not solve every problem in every circumstance. Like every Spark in this book, it should be used judiciously. When utilising pattern recognition in strategic thinking, you should beware of the following:

- **Historical bias:** Relying heavily on past patterns can lead to biases and cause you to overlook novel or emerging trends. It's important not to assume that future events will *always* mirror the past.

- **Over-reliance on data:** Excessive focus on quantifiable data might neglect qualitative factors, such as changing consumer sentiments or unquantifiable market dynamics, which can be equally critical.

- **Pattern overfitting:** There's a risk of over-interpreting data, seeing patterns where none exist, or applying patterns too rigidly, which can lead to flawed conclusions and strategies.

- **Resistance to change:** A strong focus on established patterns can create resistance to change, hindering innovation and adaptability in rapidly evolving environments.

- **Over-simplification:** Simplifying complex scenarios into recognisable patterns can result in missing nuanced factors or interactions that are crucial for comprehensive strategic planning.

- **Complacency:** Relying on pattern recognition might create a false sense of security and lead you to underestimating the need for proactive, innovative thinking in dynamic or uncertain situations.

For me pattern recognition is my intuitive gut first call. It gives me a set of directions to explore, but I often have to go a little deeper with other Sparks.

✂️ Capability-building tools & techniques

For those keen to harness pattern recognition, here are some techniques to help build that muscle:

- **Strategic journaling:** Regularly write down strategic observations and questions, reviewing them to spot recurring themes affecting decisions.

- **Mentorship:** Learn from a mentor skilled in strategic thinking for insights and guidance on recognising and utilising patterns.

- **Neuropsychological assessments:** Use tests to evaluate and enhance your pattern recognition abilities.

- **Mindfulness practices:** Engage in mindfulness and meditation to improve focus and awareness, aiding in pattern detection.

- **Critical thinking education:** Enrol in critical thinking courses to question assumptions and analyse information, boosting pattern recognition.

- **Practise:** Regularly dedicate time to observe and identify patterns in everyday life, enhancing awareness and skill in pattern making.

These methods are effective in developing a more nuanced and adept approach to strategic thinking, particularly in pattern recognition.

CASE STUDY
LIFELINE AUSTRALIA

I do a lot of work in both the health and mental health space. One significant contributor in Australia is Lifeline, which works in the complex and ever-changing field of crisis support and suicide prevention. Lifeline found itself facing some difficult challenges. The organisation was dealing with an overwhelming number of calls, but had a limited understanding of the dynamics behind them. Yes, this was a systems and data issue, but the solution is where the utility of pattern recognition came into play.

Lifeline started by analysing its extensive data on calls and caller behaviour. It quickly identified that certain times of the day had increased activity and that specific language used by callers was a clear indicator of immediate need. By recognising these patterns, Lifeline was able to optimise its staffing during high-traffic times and create a rapid response protocol for high-risk calls. The results were impressive: Lifeline increased its call-handling efficiency by over thirty per cent and improved the accuracy of its interventions.

An important aspect of this tale is that in understanding this pattern, there was also work undertaken to understand the context within which Lifeline was working. Would it change moving forward or would it stay the same? Remember, while patterns from the past help us understand and craft intuitive solutions, we can only rely on those intuitive solutions if the context is roughly the same.

📖 Resources and references

To learn more, check these out:

Barabási, Albert-László. *Linked: The New Science of Networks.* Cambridge: Perseus Publishing, 2002.

Boccaletti, Stefano, et al. *The Structure and Dynamics of Multilayer Networks.* Oxford: Oxford University Press, 2014.

Christakis, Nicholas A., and James H. Fowler. *Connected: The Surprising Power of Our Social Networks and How They Shape Our Lives.* New York: Little, Brown and Co., 2009.

Easley, David, and Jon Kleinberg. *Networks, Crowds, and Markets: Reasoning About a Highly Connected World.* New York: Cambridge University Press, 2010.

Gladwell, Malcolm. *Blink: The Power of Thinking Without Thinking.* New York: Little, Brown and Co., 2005.

Harford, Tim. *Messy: The Power of Disorder to Transform Our Lives.* New York: Riverhead Books, 2016.

Kahneman, Daniel. *Thinking, Fast and Slow.* New York: Farrar, Straus and Giroux, 2011.

Mlodinow, Leonard. *The Drunkard's Walk: How Randomness Rules Our Lives.* New York: Pantheon Books, 2008.

Taleb, Nassim Nicholas. *The Black Swan: The Impact of the Highly Improbable.* New York: Random House, 2007.

Watts, Duncan J. *Six Degrees: The Science of a Connected Age.* New York: W.W. Norton & Company, 2003.

NAVIGATING CHANGE (CH)

STAKEHOLDER ENGAGEMENT (ST)

STRATEGIC ALIGNMENT (AL)

INNOVATION & ADAPTABILITY (IN)

FINANCIAL STABILITY (FS)

CURIOSITY

CURIOSITY, OFTEN perceived as child-like wonder, is so much more than an innocent trait. It's an intrinsic force that drives us to explore the unknown, challenge our assumptions and forge new pathways. In the realm of strategic thinking, curiosity is not just a whimsical luxury; it's an absolute necessity. Einstein once said, 'I have no special talent. I am only passionately curious.' His statement underscores the importance of curiosity in driving innovation and progress.

Imagine this scenario: An interstellar organisation, known as the Galactic Curiosity Guild, is tasked with designing spacecraft. However, rather than simply enhancing the speed or fuel efficiency, it turns its focus to the deeper questions, the ones every space enthusiast has pondered. 'What lies beyond the observable universe?' 'How can we interact with cosmic phenomena in meaningful ways?'

Instead of traditional designs, its curiosity-led approach gives birth to a spacecraft equipped with advanced sensors and tools to detect and interact with unknown elements of space. This vessel isn't just a mode of transport; it's a conduit for cosmic exploration, allowing its passengers to delve deeper than ever before into the mysteries of the universe.

Such a curiosity-driven approach in the realm of outer space doesn't just lead to incremental advancements, it paves the way for groundbreaking discoveries that can redefine our understanding of the universe.

Curiosity is more than a whimsical trait found in school children and fictional detectives. It's a potent catalyst that accelerates strategic thinking and propels us towards thinking big and small. 'Curiosity is, in great and generous minds, the first passion and the last,' said Samuel Johnson. It is the desire to dig deeper, look beyond the obvious, and unshackle ourselves from preconceived notions. It's time we elevate curiosity from being a 'nice-to-have' to a critical element in strategy.

⏱ When to use this Spark

Applying curiosity will help you to excel in an environment characterised by ambiguity and complexity, when there is a lack of clear information or a need to challenge existing assumptions and norms.

Curiosity will help you solve problems that are systemic in nature, which require a holistic understanding and innovative approaches.

In scenarios that involve diverse stakeholders, curiosity will help to unearth varied perspectives and hidden insights.

Where conventional solutions have failed, curiosity prompts a re-examination of the status quo, leading to novel strategies that can break through previous barriers.

In environments that are rapidly changing, curiosity fosters a proactive approach, enabling organisations to anticipate and adapt to new challenges and opportunities, rather than merely reacting to them.

In essence, curiosity is a powerful tool for solving problems that are not just intricate but also evolving, requiring a dynamic and exploratory approach.

How to use this Spark

Practically, curiosity manifests in activities like brainstorming sessions where no idea is too far-fetched, or in embracing methodologies like design thinking, which hinge on empathetic understanding and creative problem-solving. It's about fostering a culture where questioning is encouraged and where strategies are formed not just within the four walls of a boardroom, but from a wide array of perspectives and insights.

To learn how to flex your curiosity muscle, let's look at a specific strategic issue: staff attraction and retention in the healthcare space. A manager might lead with attraction and retention research or resources from HR and the People and Culture domain. A curious strategic thinker would dive below this layer. Their thinking would follow a question and answer format, and go something like this:

Q: When people leave or stay away, what pain are they feeling or what value do they seek that we don't meet?

A: In healthcare, most of our workforce have families. Many have school age kids. By the time they get to work they are stressed by the pre-work morning duties.

Q: Why?

A: Kids are hard to get out the door and traffic is especially stressful around schools.

Q: Why do they drop them off?

A: One reason is because they are worried about them getting there safely.

You would do a lot more asking before moving into solution thinking, but when that was done, the thinking would continue like this:

Q: How can I get the kids to school with fewer cars? (we are generating options)

A: Ride sharing/organise a school bus that services a few schools/don't send them to school at all/take them early and use care services at school . . .

Q: What can I read and who can I talk to in order to find other solutions? (we are going below surface options and through engagement and testing options)

A: Okay, so what if we skewed the start times for those with families outside peak ... maybe this would help people with this stress and they will value that enough to sway their choices around staying with us.

The outcomes of using this Spark

The power of curiosity in strategy is in its ability to unearth insights that lie buried under layers of conventional thought. Curiosity unlocks a realm of practical benefits, including:

- **A learning-oriented approach:** When faced with problems or challenges, a curious mind doesn't just see obstacles; it sees puzzles waiting to be solved. This perspective shift means that instead of dreading challenges or avoiding them, a curious strategist seeks them out, eager to learn and grow from the experience.

- **Deeper stakeholder connections:** By engaging with genuine inquisitiveness, we uncover layers of insights that often remain hidden under conventional methods. This leads to strategies that resonate more deeply, are more nuanced, and are ultimately more effective because they are rooted in the authentic needs and aspirations of those we serve.

- **Greater innovation:** Curiosity encourages us to venture beyond the beaten path, to question the accepted norms and to think laterally. In a rapidly evolving world where change is the only constant, relying on old strategies or tried-and-true methods can be a recipe for obsolescence. Curiosity ensures that you're always looking out for the next big thing, always ready to adapt and evolve.

- **More resilience:** Curiosity equips organisations with the mindset to not only face uncertainties, but to embrace them as opportunities for learning and growth. This resilience is crucial in navigating the complex and often unpredictable terrain of social change.

Curiosity in strategic thinking provides a driving force that ensures that strategies are not just effective, but also innovative and forward-thinking. It's what ensures that instead of merely reacting to changes, a strategist anticipates them. It's what transforms challenges into opportunities and failures into learning experiences.

⚠ Dangers to beware of

While curiosity is a powerful tool in strategic thinking, there are certain tendencies that curiosity can produce that you should watch out for:

- **Overextension:** Excessive curiosity can lead to a scattering of focus, where too many avenues are explored simultaneously. This can dilute efforts and resources, leading to a lack of depth in any single area. It's crucial to balance exploration with focus.

- **Analysis paralysis:** An overly curious approach might result in endless questioning and analysis, delaying decision-making. In some situations, particularly in crises or when quick action is needed, this can be counterproductive.

- **Losing sight of the core mission:** In pursuit of novel ideas and approaches, there's a risk of straying too far from the core mission and values of an organisation. It's important to ensure that curiosity aligns with and supports fundamental goals.

- **Stakeholder overload:** While engaging stakeholders is crucial, excessive solicitation of input, especially without clear purpose, can lead to stakeholder fatigue. This may result in disengagement or frustration among key contributors.

- **Misalignment with resources:** Curiosity-driven initiatives need to be balanced with available resources. Pursuing too many innovative ideas without adequate resources can strain an organisation, both financially and operationally.

By being aware of these potential pitfalls, the power of curiosity can be harnessed effectively, ensuring it serves as a catalyst for innovative and impactful strategic thinking, rather than a hindrance.

⚒ Capability-building tools & techniques

Leveraging an understanding of curiosity as a linchpin for strategic advancement demands more than traditional approaches. Here are six innovative tools and ways to elevate your grasp of this concept:

- **Interactive learning platforms:** Use platforms like CuriosityStream or MasterClass for engaging, inquisitive learning experiences.

- **Escape rooms:** Participate in escape rooms to enhance critical thinking and problem-solving skills.

- **Open-ended gaming:** Engage with sandbox games like *Minecraft* to develop adaptability and creativity.

- **Curiosity-driven journaling:** End journal entries with questions to cultivate a habit of deeper inquiry.

- **Cross-disciplinary study groups:** Join diverse study groups to encourage innovative, multi-perspective thinking.

- **Virtual reality exploration:** Use VR for immersive learning experiences, expanding knowledge and sparking curiosity.

These unconventional tools and approaches not only enhance one's understanding of curiosity, but also offer ways to embed it into daily routines. As with any skill, the more it's practised, the more intrinsic it becomes.

CASE STUDY
THE CURIOUS CASE OF COMMUNITY UPLIFTMENT

A nonprofit organisation I worked with in Melbourne focused on community engagement. It realised its initiatives were becoming stagnant. Its attempts to engage the local community weren't resonating as they once did. To reinvigorate its approach, it pivoted to a curiosity-driven framework.

It initiated an 'Ask the Community' campaign, a straightforward but potent strategy: what did the community members want to know or learn? From understanding digital platforms to unravelling Indigenous Australian art, the thirst for knowledge was palpable. The nonprofit responded by organising workshops, webinars and community meet-ups to better understand and then devise community-led solutions addressing this thirst.

In a year, not only did its community engagement numbers soar, but it also found volunteers from within the community: individuals who had attended sessions and were now eager to share their knowledge and skills. By tapping into the collective curiosity of the community, the organisation not only re-established its relevance but became a fulcrum for community-driven learning and sharing.

📖 Resources and references

For those keen to further explore the nexus of curiosity and strategic thinking, here's a list of resources:

Engel, Susan. *The Hungry Mind: The Origins of Curiosity in Childhood*. Harvard University Press, 2015.

Leslie, Ian. *Curious: The Desire to Know and Why Your Future Depends On It*. Basic Books, 2014.

Edge.org. https://www.edge.org/

Berger, Warren. *A More Beautiful Question: The Power of Inquiry to Spark Breakthrough Ideas*. Bloomsbury USA, 2014.

Grazer, Brian, and Charles Fishman. *The Curious Mind: The Secret to a Bigger Life*. Simon & Schuster, 2015.

The Marginalian. www.themarginalian.org

Taberner, Kathy, and Kirsten Siggins. *The Power of Curiosity: How to Have Real Conversations That Create Collaboration, Innovation and Understanding.* Morgan James Publishing, 2015.

Mugan, Jonathan. *The Curiosity Cycle: Preparing Your Child for the Ongoing Technological Explosion.* CreateSpace Independent Publishing Platform, 2012.

Livio, Mario. *Why?: What Makes Us Curious.* Simon & Schuster, 2017.

STAKEHOLDER ENGAGEMENT (ST)

STRATEGIC ALIGNMENT (AL)

SYSTEM REFORM (SR)

GOLDEN THREAD

WHEN THINKING strategically you want to be able to tie all your thoughts, research, communications and narratives together... and *to* something. The 'golden thread' is a mental exercise that prompts you to align with and connect back to a central theme or purpose, whatever you may be thinking about or working on.

Consider a space exploration venture. The ultimate goal is to colonise Mars. This goal is so multifaceted it can easily fragment into disparate tasks like building rockets, creating life-support systems or analysing Martian soil samples. There is the danger that having so many disparate tasks to complete will cause personnel to lose sight of the common goal. So the multiple agencies involved in this life-altering journey employ the golden thread.

Using this tool, each sub-goal and task in the project is continuously vetted for its contribution to the mission of colonising Mars. The propulsion team's objective is not merely to build a rocket; it's to build a rocket that can sustain human life for the journey to Mars. The scientists are not just analysing soil; they're determining the viability of life sustenance on the planet. In a milieu where every component is profoundly complex, the golden thread serves as an anchoring element that ensures each part is a step towards the larger mission. In undertaking a project as revolutionary as colonising another planet, every small task undertaken must be in alignment with the larger mission.

The golden thread of strategy isn't just a poetic turn of phrase; it's a tangible thinking discipline that can light the path in the darkest of strategic and complex mazes. Think of it as the backbone of your strategy, a sorting filter and a unifying element that aligns all the thinking. It prevents you from diluting your efforts and wandering aimlessly, especially when the landscape is foggy and uncertain.

The golden thread is inextricable from the concept of alignment. When we talk about alignment, we refer to a systemic consistency, a harmonisation of mission, objectives, actions and measurements. Using this framework properly creates an organisational alignment so resilient it can withstand turbulence from market fluctuations or internal disruptions.

But application of the golden thread is not about arriving at a utopian state of perfect alignment. Rather, it's about establishing a dynamic equilibrium that enables you to adjust strategies and objectives without losing sight of your ultimate goal. It ensures that every operational decision, every project initiated, every metric used for performance evaluation, is a stitch in the fabric of your organisation's larger tapestry.

🕐 When to use this Spark

In essence, the golden thread is a versatile tool, valuable in ensuring strategic coherence and focus across a range of scenarios, particularly where alignment, clarity and purposeful action are crucial.

Use the golden thread when seeking alignment across the organisation. This is particularly relevant in complex organisations where activities and teams can become siloed.

The golden thread will help you during times of change or transformation to help maintain focus on the core mission.

Deploy this Spark when assessing new opportunities, investment or partnerships to determine how they align with and contribute to your organisation's strategic objectives.

When communicating strategy internally and externally, this Spark will help in clearly articulating strategy to stakeholders.

When setting up performance indicators and evaluating outcomes, the golden thread ensures that these metrics are directly tied to strategic objectives.

Employ it when brainstorming and developing solutions to challenges, ensuring that new ideas and approaches are strategically aligned.

When does the golden thread rise above other strategic concepts? Consider frameworks like SWOT analysis or balanced scorecard; these are powerful tools for situational analysis and performance measurement, but they often miss out on the integration and alignment aspect.

How to use this Spark

There are two levels to this Spark. The first is about alignment, and the second is about projection. Let's start with alignment.

1. Alignment

When you're about to bid for a new tendered service, chase that stunning merger, diversify, or invest in a new project or opportunity, ask the question: 'How does this new endeavour align with the golden thread that unifies our activities and mission?'

Try writing the key inputs to, activities in, and outputs of this new opportunity. Then convince people in your workplace how these three things line up to your purpose and mission AND how you will integrate the inputs, activities and processes into your workplace.

If all that sings, then you have a golden thread narrative and you have passed the alignment level.

2. Projection

The deeper strategic thinker mentally puts themselves in the shoes of an archer, looking down the shaft of the arrow and out onto the range. The arrow is your aligned golden thread narrative (from Step 1). The question now is: 'What can I see or anticipate because I have this alignment; what is in my new range of vision?'

Let me flesh this out with an example. Let's say you're the CEO of an organisation that is addressing youth homelessness. You build studios to go in families' backyards, and in doing so address overcrowding at home. The government asks if you would be willing to distribute education vouchers to keep kids at school—a great indicator of keeping them off the streets. How does this fit with the levels of the golden thread in action?

- **Level 1 Alignment:** Distributing education vouchers complements the accommodation aspect of your mission and purpose, and they can be distributed as part of your routine engagement around the accommodation. Also, the evidence tells you that accommodation and education work well together in this context.

- **Level 2 Projection:** Now that you are tackling these two elements, what else can you distribute or do? Food? Counselling? Connection?

One of my mottos in strategy is 'Two benefits for every move.' This is a great example of tapping into this motto to find your Level 2 benefit.

☑ The outcomes of using this Spark

The golden thread in strategic thinking refers to a clear, coherent link between an organisation's vision, strategies and operational actions. This approach ensures that every strategic decision and action is aligned with the overarching goals, leading to several practical outcomes:

- **Enhanced focus and clarity:** By maintaining a golden thread, organisations can ensure all efforts are directed towards their core objectives. This clarity of purpose helps in prioritising initiatives and resources, reducing wastage and increasing efficiency.

- **Improved stakeholder alignment:** Using this Spark facilitates alignment among stakeholders, including employees, partners and beneficiaries. When everyone understands how their contributions tie into the broader vision, it fosters a sense of unity and purpose, enhancing collaboration and commitment.

- **Increased accountability:** This approach establishes clear links between objectives and actions, making it easier to track progress and hold individuals and teams accountable for their results. It enables more effective performance monitoring and management.

- **Better decision-making:** A golden thread provides a consistent framework for decision-making. It ensures that short-term decisions are not made in isolation but are instead viewed through the lens of long-term strategic objectives.

- **Enhanced adaptability:** In rapidly changing environments, the golden thread allows organisations to adapt more effectively. While tactics might change in response to external factors, the underlying strategic objectives remain constant, providing a stable foundation for agile adaptation.

'Strategy without tactics is the slowest route to victory. Tactics without strategy is the noise before defeat,' goes the oft-quoted wisdom of Sun Tzu. The golden thread seamlessly ties strategy to tactics, ensuring that your operations are not just a series of disjointed activities, but a concerted effort to fulfil a grander purpose.

⚠ Dangers to beware of

When implementing the golden thread in strategic thinking, it's important to be mindful of certain pitfalls:

- **Over-simplification:** While clarity is a strength, oversimplifying complex issues to fit the golden thread narrative can lead to missing out on important subtleties and nuances. It's crucial to balance clarity with the complexity of real-world challenges.

- **Rigidity:** The golden thread approach could become too rigid, stifling creativity and innovation. It's essential to maintain some flexibility to adapt to unexpected changes or new opportunities.

- **Misalignment:** There's a risk of misinterpreting or incorrectly implementing the golden thread, leading to strategies and actions that deviate from the intended vision and goals. Continuous alignment checks are necessary.

- **Neglect of external factors:** Focusing too intently on internal alignment might lead to neglecting external changes and trends. It's important to keep an outward-looking perspective to ensure the strategy remains relevant and responsive.

- **Limited perspective:** The golden thread must be inclusive of diverse perspectives and insights. A narrow view could lead to strategies that are not fully informed or comprehensive.

Being aware of and actively managing these potential challenges is key to leveraging the golden thread approach effectively in strategic planning.

⚒ Capability-building tools & techniques

Here are some tools to help build your strategic thinking muscle around the golden thread:

- **Narrative workshops:** Conduct storytelling workshops to integrate the golden thread into your organisational narratives.

- **Digital storyboards:** Use tools like Storyboard That or Miro for visualising strategic plans, highlighting the golden thread's role.

- **Case studies:** Develop case studies focusing on how the golden thread influenced successes and learnings.

- **Role-playing:** Implement role-playing to explore the golden thread's impact in various scenarios.

- **Strategic fiction writing:** Craft stories projecting your organisation's future with the golden thread as a key element.

- **Interactive story mapping:** Blend interactive elements into journey mapping, exploring decisions aligned with the golden thread.

These techniques place storytelling at the heart of strategy, transforming the golden thread from a concept into a practical, visible tool across your organisation.

⌕ CASE STUDY
FEEDING FUTURES

Feeding Futures, a nonprofit organisation with a vision to eradicate child hunger, found itself grappling with diverse projects—from educational programs and community outreach to meal distribution and fundraising campaigns. The challenge wasn't the lack of enthusiasm or resources; it was the lack of a unifying strategic thread that connected all these functions to the ultimate goal of the organisation: eradicating child hunger.

Feeding Futures implemented the golden thread approach to infuse every project, every decision and every metric with a sense of purpose tied directly back to the mission. The transformation was nearly instant. Teams that were previously siloed began to collaborate, not because they were told to, but because they realised their activities were different chapters in the same story. The fundraising team, for example, not only focused on raising funds but on ensuring that the collected resources would directly contribute to either educating communities on nutrition or funding meals for children in need. The program designers started structuring educational content that wasn't just informational but transformative, equipping communities to contribute to the mission.

In a year, Feeding Futures saw a forty per cent increase in overall mission effectiveness, measured not just in funds raised or meals distributed, but in long-term sustainable impacts like improved community awareness and reduced child malnutrition rates. By consistently adhering to the golden thread, Feeding Futures transformed itself into an organisation that was not just doing good but was also effective and aligned.

📖 Resources and references

The golden thread of strategy has been explored in various forms: through books, articles and podcasts that offer both conceptual frameworks and case studies. Here are some references to deepen your understanding:

Kaplan, Robert S., and David P. Norton. *The Balanced Scorecard: Translating Strategy into Action*. Boston: Harvard Business School Press, 1996.

Kim, W. Chan, and Renée Mauborgne. *Blue Ocean Strategy: How to Create Uncontested Market Space and Make Competition Irrelevant*. Boston: Harvard Business Review Press, 2005.

Ries, Eric. *The Lean Startup: How Today's Entrepreneurs Use Continuous Innovation to Create Radically Successful Businesses*. New York: Crown Business, 2011.

Rumelt, Richard. *Good Strategy, Bad Strategy: The Difference and Why It Matters*. New York: Crown Business, 2011.

Osterwalder, Alexander, and Yves Pigneur. *Business Model Generation: A Handbook for Visionaries, Game Changers, and Challengers*. New Jersey: John Wiley & Sons, 2010.

Porter, Michael E. *Competitive Strategy: Techniques for Analyzing Industries and Competitors*. New York: Free Press, 1980.

Senge, Peter M. *The Fifth Discipline: The Art & Practice of the Learning Organization*. New York: Doubleday, 1990.

The Strategy Skills Podcast.

Taleb, Nassim Nicholas. *Antifragile: Things That Gain from Disorder*. New York: Random House, 2012.

STAKEHOLDER ENGAGEMENT (ST)

STRATEGIC ALIGNMENT (AL)

CULTURE & LEADERSHIP (CL)

KINDNESS

I BET you weren't expecting to see a section on kindness in a book like this. But let's consider what we mean by kindness in a strategic context. It's not about being the doormat of your stakeholders or indiscriminately saying yes to everything. Rather, it's an approach that puts human values at the core of decision-making. Kindness in strategy means operating in a way that is fundamentally respectful and considerate to the human beings involved, whether they're employees, customers or community members. It's about creating a culture that prioritises humane outcomes, one where stakeholder well-being is not just an agenda item, but is ingrained in every strategic objective.

Imagine you're commanding a spaceship, the USS *Empathy*, and you're on a mission to establish the first intergalactic colony. You've got a multi-species crew, cutting-edge technology and a well-defined mission plan. You're light years away from Earth, but your strategy is grounded in something deeply human: kindness.

The different species on board have disparate needs and priorities. A hive-mind species is focused on collective well-being, while a silicon-based life form cares primarily about data and energy conservation. These differences can be your downfall or your strength, and kindness becomes your strategic edge. In this context, kindness isn't a triviality; it's a fundamental strategy.

By adopting an ethos of kindness, you understand the unique conditions needed for each life form to thrive. You modify the ship's environmental settings not just for optimal human comfort, but for the varied biologies on board. When allocating resources, you ensure equitable distribution, considering the specific needs of each species. Kindness breeds an environment of respect and collaboration and, soon enough, your diverse crew is innovating, finding synergies that a more self-centred approach would have missed.

Remember, outer space is harsh and unforgiving. A strategy based on kindness becomes your life-support system, a way to ensure that the 'human' elements—trust, collaboration and morale—are in abundant supply when you're galaxies away from home. It's not just a 'nice-to-have'; it's mission-critical.

It's easy to think that kindness is an outdated concept. At the time of writing, the Russian 'special operation' in Ukraine was 600 days old, Israel was at war with Hamas, and Australians had just voted 'No' to a national referendum on establishing an Aboriginal Voice to Parliament.

But it seems to me that no matter what strategic sense you use, kindness needs to be in the frame. By embedding kindness into your strategic thinking, you're not just checking a box on corporate social responsibility or 'woke' culture. You're making a lasting investment in the sustainability and effectiveness of your strategy. Let's challenge the conventional wisdom and see how an element as 'soft' as kindness can play a crucial role in something as 'hard' as strategy.

When to use this Spark

When do you deploy kindness as a strategic concept? The answer is almost counterintuitive: when things get tough. When you're faced with budget constraints, talent attrition or stakeholder scepticism, kindness can be the glue that holds your strategic objectives together.

But is kindness always the superior strategic choice? Not necessarily. There are contexts where other strategic principles like efficiency, innovation or rapid growth may take precedence. However, kindness becomes the most superior choice when you find that your organisation needs more than just a roadmap to reach an objective. It needs the collective will, the emotional investment and the resilience that comes from feeling valued and respected.

▦ How to use this Spark

Isn't it interesting that I need to even write this down? As humans we are wired to be connected and a key to connection is trust. Kindness is a driver of trust . . . so why isn't kindness just a default in our thinking? Well, my new friend, I blame capitalism and the patriarchy . . . but don't get me started on that just yet!

Now, I'm sure you're a kind person, but it's possible to overlook this factor in strategic thinking. Try the following exercise to put it back at the centre of your strategy.

To my mind, deploying kindness in your thinking takes a step beyond understanding and delivering and arrives at a true value proposition. If you are used to understanding what consumers value and then developing products and services to meet this value, then you will be using many of the same tools here.

In order to embed kindness, we need to develop empathy for those we seek to help and identify what elements inside this empathy we can and should address. To do this, try these steps:

1 Prepare yourself by thinking: 'This activity is not about me, my workplace or the capabilities we have. It's about understanding the people we wish to help—deeply.'

2 Identify the people at the centre of the matter. Not just by broad categories, but by profiling them. To do this, lean on any one of the free profiling templates available online.

3   Develop an empathy map for each profile. An empathy map is another tool that is widely available online. It helps us understand what people are thinking and feeling in their daily lives, what they hear, what they see, and what they say and do.

4   With this understanding we can then develop a sense of what people are trying to get done, what they hope to gain by completing these activities, and what pains they experience when undertaking these activities.

5   In other Sparks you will focus on the value you can create for people, but here the focus is on kindness. So, with this information at hand, ask yourself the following questions:

   a   If there was an act of service or a kindness we could perform for these people, that was not a funded service or transaction, what would it be and why would we do it?

   b   If I could adjust our services to include an act of kindness, would it drive more impact— would it help more?

   c   If we could re-organise all the services, service providers and policy wonks around a system that delivered to kindness as the major goal, what would be the key changes we would make?

6   Bring it back together into a holistic map by scribbling your thoughts onto a whiteboard.

7   Develop a narrative and a strategic response based on this kindness work.

☑ The outcomes of using this Spark

I believe that using kindness in strategic thinking leads to many practical outcomes, including:

- **Enhanced employee engagement:** You will find that kindness fosters a supportive work environment, increasing job satisfaction and productivity as people connect at a human level to purpose and mission.

- **Stronger stakeholder connection:** Connecting outside your workplace becomes more intuitive and easier when you discuss kindness. It helps build trust and long-lasting partnerships through empathetic and understanding interactions.

- **Improved loyalty:** You might be surprised at the way consumers attach to your workplace when they see and feel kindness at play.

- **More ethical decisions:** Kindness is a great shortcut for those new to embedding a moral compass into work. It guides socially responsible and fair practices, aligning with today's value-driven consumer and employee expectations.

- **Competitive differentiation:** There is no doubt your workplace will be positioned differently. We are far too clinical in how we design and deliver services—this is particularly true in the nonprofit space, probably due to how the sector is funded. Kindness will provide a unique edge in a noisy market by resonating on a human level.

- **Smoother waters in disruptive times:** You might be surprised how putting the consumer and kindness back into the centre of any view can help resolve conflict inside and outside the workplace. A kind approach in strategy can de-escalate conflicts and promote harmonious resolutions when tension is present.

- **Innovation and growth:** Kindness opens up new thinking pathways and activates a different lens for us to tackle our work. It creates a safe space for creativity and risk-taking.

Kindness by default in strategic thinking embeds a real human-centred flavour to your insights and, in the end, it is this human centricity that will lead to the enduring success of what you set out to do.

⚠ Dangers to beware of

When applying kindness in strategic thinking, it's important to be aware of certain pitfalls:

- **Overemphasis on harmony:** Prioritising kindness shouldn't lead to avoiding necessary tough decisions or constructive conflicts that drive innovation and progress.

- **Perception of weakness:** There's a risk that kindness may be misconstrued as a lack of assertiveness or firmness, especially in competitive business environments.

- **Compromised business objectives:** Kindness must be balanced with practical business goals. It's crucial not to compromise on key strategic objectives in the pursuit of kindness.

- **Potential for exploitation:** In some cases, kindness can be taken advantage of, so it's essential to couple it with discernment and clear boundaries.

- **Scepticism:** Kindness should be authentic and consistently applied; otherwise, it can lead to scepticism and cynicism among employees and stakeholders.

- **Misalignment with organisational culture:** If an organisation's culture isn't supportive of kindness as a value, implementing it as a strategic approach can face significant resistance.

By being mindful of these challenges, kindness can be effectively integrated into strategic thinking in a way that enhances relationships, culture and outcomes without compromising on business acumen and effectiveness.

Capability-building tools & techniques

Here are some methods that can be integrated into your daily life and strategic thinking to truly become a kinder individual and organisation. The payoff? Enhanced relationships, a more positive organisational culture and, quite often, more effective solutions to complex problems:

- **Empathy maps:** Use various templates available online to better understand others' perspectives.

- **Mindfulness:** Practise being present and emotionally aware, making kindness more natural.

- **Compassion circles:** Share experiences in a supportive environment, focusing on listening to build empathy.

- **Kindness journal:** Document and reflect on acts of kindness to reinforce this behaviour in daily life.

- **Stakeholder empathy mapping:** Identify specific needs and opportunities for kindness in your interactions with teams, clients and the community.

- **Conflict resolution practice:** Prepare for conflicts and use them as chances to demonstrate kindness and foster growth.

- **Socratic dialogues:** Engage in discussions about complex issues to enhance understanding and kindness towards diverse perspectives.

I know, many of these may seem a bit odd in a strategic thinking book; however, they do speak to one of my underlying philosophies—we must re-integrate our humanity and bring our whole selves if we are to function (and think) better.

🔍 CASE STUDY
MAXIMISING KINDNESS TO TRANS-FORM COMMUNITY WELL-BEING

When 'HarmonyHaven', a nonprofit focused on mental health, incorporated kindness as a key strategy, the results were palpable. The leadership team recognised the growing societal divide and set out to build an ethos around empathy and respect.

Within a year, volunteer engagement doubled. Volunteers weren't just showing up; they were passionately contributing to HarmonyHaven's mission. The organisation began offering programs in stress management, counselling services and educational workshops—all free of charge. By adopting kindness as a strategy, it humanised its interactions with community members, breaking down barriers that often prevent people from seeking mental health support.

This human touch translated into improved donor relations. When people see an organisation not merely as a service provider but as a compassionate entity, they're more willing to donate. Funding increased by forty per cent, allowing HarmonyHaven to extend its services and reach. Perhaps most astonishing was the twenty-five per cent decrease in community-reported mental health incidents. By deploying kindness, the nonprofit not only improved its internal workings, but had a transformative impact on the community it served.

📖 Resources and references

Here is your serving of deep dive resources:

Brown, Brené. *Daring Greatly: How the Courage to Be Vulnerable Transforms the Way We Live, Love, Parent, and Lead.* Penguin Random House, 2012.

Gilbert, Paul. *The Compassionate Mind.* New Harbinger Publications, 2009.

Goetz, Jennifer L., Dacher Keltner, and Emiliana Simon-Thomas. 'Compassion: An Evolutionary Analysis and Empirical Review.' *Psychological Bulletin,* 2010.

Keltner, Dacher. *Born to Be Good: The Science of a Meaningful Life.* W.W. Norton & Company, 2009.

Neff, Kristin. *Self-Compassion: The Proven Power of Being Kind to Yourself.* HarperCollins, 2011.

Post, Stephen G., and Jill Neimark. *Why Good Things Happen to Good People: The Exciting New Research That Proves the Link Between Doing Good and Living a Longer, Healthier, Happier Life.* Random House, 2007.

Ricard, Matthieu. *Happiness: A Guide to Developing Life's Most Important Skill.* Little, Brown and Co., 2006.

Schwartz, Tony. *The Way We're Working Isn't Working.* Free Press, 2010.

Seligman, Martin E.P. *Authentic Happiness: Using the New Positive Psychology to Realize Your Potential for Lasting Fulfillment.* Free Press, 2002.

Thich Nhat Hanh. *The Miracle of Mindfulness: An Introduction to the Practice of Meditation.* Beacon Press, 1999.

RESOURCE MANAGEMENT (RE)

INNOVATION & ADAPTABILITY (IN)

SYSTEM REFORM (SR)

RISK MANAGEMENT (RI)

TIMING— STRATEGY'S X FACTOR

TIMING, IN its most basic definition, is the selection of the best moment to take an action. In the realm of strategy, it's the art and science of knowing when to make your move, and, just as importantly, when not to. It's a delicate balance between preparation and opportunity. As Sun Tzu eloquently wrote in *The Art of War*, 'Opportunities multiply as they are seized.' This isn't just about seizing them; it's about discerning when to seize them.

Consider this... In the distant Andromeda system, Commander Zara helmed the starship *Odyssey*, a vessel on a critical mission for Earth's Intergalactic Council. Her task was to negotiate a trade treaty with the elusive Zentari race.

The Zentari, known for their precise and ritualistic nature, valued timing above all. Any diplomatic move, if not timed perfectly with their complex celestial calendar, would be seen as a grave disrespect, dooming the talks before they began.

Commander Zara, well-versed in strategic nuances, synchronised every aspect of the mission with the Zentari's calendar. From the timing of hyperspace jumps to the delivery of communication bursts, each action was meticulously planned and executed.

The *Odyssey*'s approach to the Zentari home world was timed to coincide with the zenith of their Great Star, a sacred event. As the star reached its peak, Zara initiated the first diplomatic transmission, aligning her greeting with the Zentari's high observance.

The Zentari, impressed by this display of respect and understanding, welcomed the *Odyssey*'s crew. The ensuing talks, held in the harmonious afterglow of the Great Star, were successful, leading to a historic alliance.

Commander Zara's strategic acumen in leveraging timing not only averted potential conflict but also ushered in a new era of trade and cooperation, showcasing that in the infinite web of interstellar relations, timing is indeed everything.

In the annals of strategic thinking, this factor often receives less attention than it should. In writing this I debated whether to rank these strategic thinking elements. If I had done so, I'm pretty sure this element would have been in the top three.

The benefits of nailing strategic timing are profound. It amplifies reach, optimises resource utilisation, and can be the difference between success and fading into obscurity. A perfect example is Netflix's transition from DVD rentals to streaming, timed impeccably with advancements in internet speed and accessibility.

In the world of for-purpose strategy, timing isn't merely a detail—it's the foundation of impact. In the vast constellation of stakeholders, missions and goals that make up this sector, the alignment of these elements at the right moment can catalyse unprecedented transformations. Just as the gravitational pull of celestial bodies influences their motion and timing, the pulse and needs of our communities should guide our strategic moves.

While all elements of strategy are important, timing trumps many because of its amplifying effect. The most brilliant strategy, if executed too early or too late, loses its lustre.

When to use this Spark

Every strategic decision has a timing element. From choosing when to enter a market, to timing a rebrand, or deciding the right moment to pivot. As society, technology and global events shift and evolve at rapid paces, timing decisions become even more important.

So, when should one incorporate timing into strategic considerations? While there are times when timing is especially critical, the short answer is: **always**.

How to use this Spark

There are two streams of 'timing' thinking. The first is preparing yourself so that when the time is right, you can act. The second is taking advantage of unforeseen opportunities. I think the second is really an accelerated version of the first, so I have stepped the first out here.

To practically implement the Spark of timing in strategic thinking, follow these steps:

1. **Create your success criteria:** Develop a clear and defensible view on 'what good looks like'. If all these conditions are met, then it's the best time to act.

2. **Set your baseline:**

   a. **Market analysis:** Begin with a thorough analysis of market trends and patterns. Understand the cycles, seasonal fluctuations and consumer behaviours that could impact your strategy.

   b. **Industry, sector or segment monitoring:** Use a tool like Porter's five forces (an oldie but a goodie: https://hbr.org/2008/01/the-five-competitive-forces-that-shape-strategy) to help you make sure you can see all the actors in your sector. Keep a close watch on actors. Anticipate their moves and plan your timing accordingly.

c **Internal readiness assessment:** Ensure your organisation is ready to act. This involves aligning resources, preparing teams and setting up necessary processes.

3 **Create your triggers** (don't go overboard, keep it tight, keep it simple). These include:

a A view on where you are now against each element in the success criteria.

b A way to be alerted if things change and move closer to your success criteria.

c A set of actions to take when one of your conditions is triggered.

4 **Develop your stakeholder engagement plan:** Consider the best time to engage stakeholders. Timing your communications and actions to align with their expectations and readiness can significantly boost support and success.

5 **Conduct a risk assessment:** Evaluate the risks associated with timing. Consider potential market changes, competitor reactions and internal capabilities to mitigate risks.

6 **Develop your 'Go':** Have your plan ready to hit the 'Go' button so you can just get into the doing once your success criteria are triggered.

7 **Create a feedback loop:** Establish a feedback mechanism so you can do it better next time.

These steps might sound like a lot, but will start to just flow in your mega mind after some practise. And by following these steps, you can effectively integrate timing into your strategic planning, ensuring that your actions are not only well planned, but also executed at the most opportune moments for maximum impact.

☑ The outcomes of using this Spark

Incorporating timing into strategic thinking yields several practical outcomes essential for success in any sector:

- **Enhanced decision-making:** By understanding the optimal timing for actions, you can capitalise on opportunities and avoid pitfalls. This leads to improved efficiency and effectiveness in achieving strategic goals.

- **Better resource allocation:** Strategically timed actions ensure resources are used when they are most impactful, maximising return on investment and reducing waste.

- **Better strategic positioning:** Mastery of timing can provide a significant competitive advantage. Anticipating market shifts and competitor moves can help to outmanoeuvre rivals and capture market share.

- **Improved stakeholder engagement:** Releasing information, launching products or initiating changes at the right moment can significantly impact stakeholder reception and support, crucial for the success of any strategy.

- **Better risk management:** Understanding the temporal aspects of risks enables proactive mitigation and better preparedness for potential challenges.

In essence, integrating timing into strategic thinking is not just about when to act, but understanding the ripple effects of these actions through the lens of opportunity, resource optimisation, competition, stakeholder dynamics and risk management, all of which are pivotal for strategic success.

⚠ Dangers to beware of

When using timing in strategic thinking, be wary of these potential pitfalls:

- **Analysis paralysis:** Over-focusing on timing can lead to indecision and missed opportunities.

- **Misjudgement of market signals:** Incorrect timing can result in strategic errors or wasted resources.

- **Neglect of other elements:** Don't let timing overshadow other critical factors like content quality or stakeholder engagement.

- **Over-reliance on historical data:** Past patterns don't always predict future scenarios; stay adaptive to current trends.

- **Misalignment of elements:** Ensure synchronisation between various strategic components for effective implementation.

- **Underestimation of external factors:** Be aware of external market conditions and competitor movements that can impact your timing.

- **Ignoring stakeholder readiness:** Timing should align with the readiness and receptiveness of stakeholders.

- **Lack of flexibility:** Maintain flexibility to adjust timing as circumstances evolve.

- **Overlooked risk management:** Consider potential risks associated with timing decisions.

- **Failure to communicate:** Make sure you effectively communicate the timing aspect of your strategy internally and externally.

Acknowledging these challenges is key to successfully incorporating timing into your strategic planning, ensuring it enhances rather than hinders your strategic objectives.

⚒ Capability-building tools & techniques

Here are some ways to develop your timing Spark:

- **Scenario-planning workshops:** Engage in workshops to explore how timing affects strategic outcomes, using facilitators or software to simulate future scenarios.

- **Time-series analysis education:** Learn to predict future events by studying past trends through online courses.

- **Simulation software:** Utilise tools like AnyLogic to model business processes and assess timing impacts.

- **Competitive intelligence training:** Take courses to learn about competitor timings and adjust your strategies accordingly.

- **Mentorship:** Seek advice from industry experts with professional experience who have a proven track record in strategic timing.

These techniques will not only boost your theoretical knowledge, but also provide practical skills for effectively applying timing in your strategic decisions.

🔍 CASE STUDY
SAME-SEX MARRIAGE—TAILORING
A MESSAGE TO A MOMENT

Let's illustrate with nonprofits or rather, in this case, from the broader social sector: the journey of the same-sex marriage movement in Australia.

From the onset, advocates faced a multitude of challenges. Prior to 2004, Australia's marriage laws were ambiguous regarding same-sex unions. However, that year saw the Australian Government amend the Marriage Act to explicitly define marriage as a union between a man and a woman. This move solidified the legal barriers same-sex couples faced. It would take years of strategic campaigning, informed by impeccable timing, to reverse this.

In the decade following the 2004 amendment, same-sex marriage advocates focused on three key strategies: building broad-based public support, cultivating allies within both major political parties, and garnering international backing. By 2015, a confluence of factors suggested that the timing was ripe for a decisive push.

Firstly, the international milieu was changing. By mid-2015, nations like the United States, Canada and New Zealand had already legalised same-sex marriage. These international shifts didn't just offer a beacon of hope; they provided tangible proof that change was achievable, even in nations with political landscapes similar to Australia's.

In parallel, and within Australia, public opinion had evolved considerably. Polls indicated a clear majority in favour of same-sex marriage. The for-purpose sector and numerous nonprofits championed the cause, amplifying the voices of the LGBTQ+ community. Their tireless advocacy work ensured that the narrative of love, rights and equality resonated deeply with the broader Australian populace.

Meanwhile, in the political arena, the timing proved essential. With leadership changes in the major parties, there was an increasing appetite for revisiting the marriage debate. By aligning their push with these leadership changes, advocates ensured their cause would not be overlooked.

However, the path to legalisation was not without its hurdles. In 2017, the Turnbull government, in lieu of a straightforward parliamentary vote, opted for a postal survey to gauge public opinion. Critics argued this was a delay tactic. Nevertheless, the same-sex marriage movement, recognising the potential of this moment, mobilised en masse. The resulting campaign emphasised personal stories, focusing on love and commitment rather than just rights and legalities. The strategy proved effective. When the results were announced, 61.6 per cent of Australians voiced their support for same-sex marriage.

The timing of the movement's tactics during this postal survey was impeccable. By tailoring their message to the moment—understanding the nation's mood and the broader international context—advocates ensured overwhelming public support. This public mandate expedited the legislative process, and, by December 2017, same-sex marriage was legalised in Australia.

The trajectory of the same-sex marriage movement in Australia underscores the profound importance of timing in strategic advocacy. By adeptly navigating the intersections of public sentiment, political will and international trends, advocates transformed a once divisive issue into a unifying moment of national pride. Their success offers a masterclass in how strategic timing, underpinned by persistent advocacy, can catalyse monumental societal change.

Resources and references

For those looking to delve deeper into this topic, here are some more resources:

Pink, Daniel H. *When: The Scientific Secrets of Perfect Timing*. New York: Riverhead Books, 2018.

Barabási, Albert-László. *Linked: The New Science of Networks*. Cambridge: Perseus Publishing, 2002.

Boccaletti, Stefano, et al. *The Structure and Dynamics of Multilayer Networks*. Oxford: Oxford University Press, 2014.

Christakis, Nicholas A., and James H. Fowler. *Connected: The Surprising Power of Our Social Networks and How They Shape Our Lives*. New York: Little, Brown and Co., 2009.

Easley, David, and Jon Kleinberg. *Networks, Crowds, and Markets: Reasoning About a Highly Connected World*. New York: Cambridge University Press, 2010.

Gladwell, Malcolm. *Blink: The Power of Thinking Without Thinking.* New York: Little, Brown and Co., 2005.

Harford, Tim. *Messy: The Power of Disorder to Transform Our Lives.* New York: Riverhead Books, 2016.

Kahneman, Daniel. *Thinking, Fast and Slow.* New York: Farrar, Straus and Giroux, 2011.

Mlodinow, Leonard. *The Drunkard's Walk: How Randomness Rules Our Lives.* New York: Pantheon Books, 2008.

Taleb, Nassim Nicholas. *The Black Swan: The Impact of the Highly Improbable.* New York: Random House, 2007.

Watts, Duncan J. *Six Degrees: The Science of a Connected Age.* New York: W.W. Norton & Company, 2003.

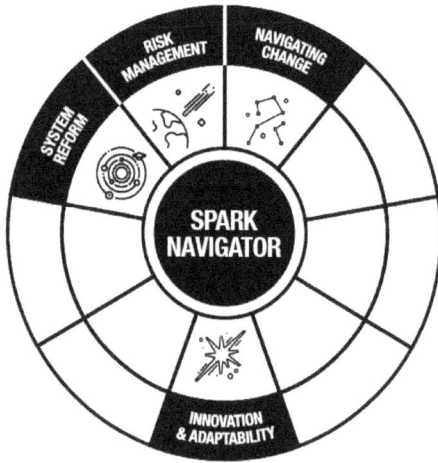

NAVIGATING CHANGE (CH)

INNOVATION & ADAPTABILITY (IN)

SYSTEM REFORM (SR)

RISK MANAGEMENT (RI)

HOLISTIC THINKING

A KEY feature of strategic thinking is that it is holistic. It embraces the whole organisation, not just its parts. Remember, 'The whole is greater than the sum of its parts.' Aristotle imparted that truism millennia ago, yet its profundity resonates more than ever in today's complex world. Mastery of this Spark is one of the foundational skills in strategic thinking. Even in outer space...

In the sprawling Eridani Sector, the Intergalactic Alliance faced a perplexing crisis on the planet Zephyria. Initially, the problem appeared to be purely environmental—a simple case of ecological mismanagement. But Commander Vega, a strategist renowned for her depth and breadth of vision, suspected there was more to the situation. Leaning into her holistic thinking skills, she took the brave step of pausing the planning in progress and stepped back to unearth the true extent of the crisis.

Delving deeper, it became clear that the issue was far more complex than first thought. The environmental degradation was a symptom, not the cause. Vega worked with both her team and the Zephyrian Council to deeply unpack the problem. They found that the root cause was an intricate web of economic policies, social drivers and political dynamics. Vega was now convinced that a singular focus on environmental repair would ultimately fail.

With this revelation, Vega assembled a diverse team of experts from various disciplines. Together, they crafted a strategy that addressed the multifaceted nature of the crisis. Environmental scientists collaborated with economic advisers to develop sustainable resource management plans that supported economic stability. Social anthropologists and political strategists worked in tandem to ensure these plans were socially equitable and politically feasible.

This holistic approach led to a series of interconnected solutions, each reinforcing the other, creating a sustainable and harmonious path forward for Zephyria. Commander Vega's success in the Eridani Sector became a galactic case study in the power of holistic thinking, illustrating how stepping back to view the broader constellation of factors can transform a strategy from a singular fix to a comprehensive solution for lasting change.

No one function inside a workplace provides all of its own inputs, does all of its own processing of these inputs, or creates all of its outputs. Other parts of the organisation, indeed partners and the ecosystem outside, can also contribute. Quickest example—you can't deliver programs without support from corporate services and an authorising environment from, say, the government.

Connection between people, teams and divisions at an atomic level is vital to value. As such, it is also vital to any strategic thinking you will do.

So when we think strategically and holistically, it's not some trite head nod to common sense.

Rather, it's a piercing understanding of how all the parts of the workplace pull together to enhance each other's efforts at the atomic level, matched with an even clearer sense of what value could and should be created to deliver more impact by all elements pulling together in new and better ways.

If it isn't holistic, it's not strategic thinking.

🕐 When to use this Spark

When should we adopt this 'whole organisation' lens in our strategic thinking? The answer is simple: always. Whether you're navigating a crisis, exploring new avenues for growth or refining existing processes, this approach offers clarity, ensuring that every decision, big or small, aligns with the broader mission.

But the holistic organisational view shines brightest **when complexity is at its peak**. In a world that's increasingly interconnected, where ripple effects can trigger tidal waves, this approach ensures resilience, adaptability and, ultimately, sustainable success.

📋 How to use this Spark

How do you go about learning this critical skill? What steps do you take to get this level of insight?

1 **Know these four things:**

   a **How change happens:** How do you, or can you, make impact happen (aka the Theory of Change)?

   b **How you work:** Unpack your operating model down to value chains so you can see the atomic makeup of how you make change happen.

   c **Where the links are:** Map out the links between your teams using whiteboards and network mapping tools.

   d **The gap of wasted aspiration:** Be realistic and map out, in plain speak, the gap between what your best possible self could look like and what you do now, and highlight disconnection and non-holistic thinking.

2 **Broaden information sources:** Actively seek diverse information sources to gain a wide range of perspectives. This includes industry reports, academic research and insights from different stakeholders to shed light on what you are and could be.

3 **Practise cross-disciplinary learning:** Engage with ideas and concepts from various disciplines. This might involve attending workshops or webinars outside your field to understand different approaches and methodologies.

4 **Stress-test:** Develop your thinking, solutions or hypothesis and test each and every gap you have identified in the previous steps to see if the outcomes could be improved by being holistic.

5 **Project outside the workplace:** Cultivate a systems thinking approach, viewing the organisation as part of a larger ecosystem and understanding how leveraging parts of the system can enhance your strategic thinking.

To clarify, let's draw a picture of where we want to end up with all this... Imagine yourself in a command centre, surrounded by a series of dials and buttons. Each dial represents a facet of your organisation or project: finance, human resources, societal impact—you name it. Now, holistic thinking is like having an extra dial labelled 'Optimal Outcome', which is connected to all the other dials. Turning it doesn't just move one or two indicators; it optimally adjusts them all, creating a harmonious balance that achieves your strategic goals without undermining any single aspect.

☑ The outcomes of using the Spark

Incorporating holistic thinking into a nonprofit's strategic planning yields several practical outcomes:

- **Comprehensive program development:** Strategies developed will encompass all facets of program impact, from direct service delivery to broader community effects.

- **Enhanced resource utilisation:** A holistic approach ensures more efficient and effective use of resources, aligning them with multiple facets of the organisation's purpose.

- **Improved stakeholder relations:** By considering the diverse needs of, and impacts on, various stakeholders, relationships with donors, volunteers and the community are strengthened.

- **Greater adaptability to change:** Holistic thinking prepares the organisation to adapt more readily to external changes by recognising interconnected external factors.

- **Sustainable impact strategies:** Strategies are more sustainable, as they consider long-term impacts and the interplay between different organisational activities and goals.

- **Increased organisational resilience:** By viewing the organisation within a larger ecosystem, strategies are more resilient to unforeseen challenges.

- **Effective risk management:** Holistic thinking leads to identifying and mitigating a broader range of risks.

One of the underlying factors that enables us to drive long-run success is being able to clearly see the whole picture and, with this understanding, anticipate and adapt to this picture. This Spark is a key tool to help you with both.

⚠ Dangers to beware of

In applying holistic thinking to a nonprofit's strategic planning, it's important to watch out for:

- **Over-complexity:** Avoid creating strategies so complex that they become impractical or difficult to communicate and implement.

- **Analysis paralysis:** Be wary of getting so caught up in considering every angle that it leads to indecision or delays in action.

- **Overstretched resources:** Ensure that striving for holistic solutions doesn't lead to overextending your organisation's resources.

- **Neglecting immediate priorities:** Balance the need for comprehensive long-term planning with addressing urgent short-term needs.

- **Attempting perfect integration:** Acknowledge that while striving for interconnected strategies is ideal, perfect integration across all organisational aspects may not always be feasible.

By being mindful of these factors, holistic thinking can effectively guide strategic planning, ensuring it remains practical, focused and aligned with the organisation's mission.

✂ Capability-building tools & techniques

To implement holistic thinking, start with these actionable steps:

- **Systems thinking courses:** To really grasp the concept of holistic thinking in strategic planning, delve into courses on systems thinking. This is essentially the academic term for holistic thinking and teaches you to see how parts interact within the whole of a system. You'll not only get frameworks, but also real-world applications that can elevate your strategy game.

- **Scenario-planning workshops:** One of the best ways to get comfortable with holistic thinking is to engage in scenario planning. Workshops can offer hands-on experience in considering multiple variables and seeing how they interconnect. You can find these workshops being offered by think tanks, universities and consulting firms.

- **Advanced strategy simulations:** Digital simulation tools, often used in MBA programs, allow you to virtually implement strategic decisions and see their cascade effects in an entire organisation or ecosystem. Some of these tools have evolved to a level of sophistication that is profoundly enlightening.

- **Peer-to-peer learning circles:** Sometimes, wisdom comes from the collective. Form or join learning circles focused on strategy and problem-solving. The multiple perspectives you'll encounter will naturally push you to think more holistically. These circles can be in-person or digital, formal or casual.

- **AI-driven analysis tools:** While not a replacement for human intuition and expertise, AI tools that can analyse massive datasets can provide insights that would be otherwise impossible or incredibly time-consuming to obtain. This analysis can help inform a more holistic view of a given strategic issue.

- **Mindfulness and cognitive flexibility training:** Holistic thinking is not just about external factors; it's also about internal cognitive processes. Training programs that focus on mindfulness and cognitive flexibility can help hone your ability to juggle multiple thoughts and consider various perspectives simultaneously.

Sorting through the world of resources that could help was difficult for this Spark. I suggest you pick one or two of the ones listed, compare to the problem or opportunity in front of you, and become proficient at that before stepping out into the other tools.

🔍 CASE STUDY
INTEGRATED FUNDRAISING
AT CARE INTERNATIONAL

In the ever-changing realm of global aid and advocacy, organisations like Care International exemplify the necessity of continual adaptation and evolution. Originating in 1945 to send 'care packages' after World War II, Care International evolved into a leading humanitarian agency. However, by the mid-2010s, challenges arose due to its siloed operations across ninety countries, each with independent agendas and initiatives. This fragmented approach hindered overall efficiency and impact.

Recognising the need for change, the leadership embarked on a strategic shift towards a more unified, organisation-wide approach. This transition began with extensive, collaborative consultations with staff globally to understand regional nuances and challenges. The integration strategy, co-created through this process, led to remarkable outcomes. In Africa, disparate regional women's empowerment programs were unified into a continent-wide initiative, significantly enhancing impact and reach. In the Americas, the merging of separate disaster relief entities resulted in a more efficient response system.

This integrated approach also revolutionised fundraising, positioning Care International as a global force, leading to larger grants and more ambitious projects. By 2020, the organisation was not just making an impact, but redefining operational standards for global nonprofits. This transformation highlights the effectiveness of thinking holistically, underscoring that the chosen approach can significantly influence the solvability of social problems.

Resources and references

Your deep dive dose:

Anzalone, Chris. 'Decentralized Ecosystems: Nurturing the Entrepreneurial Paradigm of the 21st Century'. *Medium*, 2018.

Brafman, Ori, and Rod A. Beckstrom. *The Starfish and the Spider: The Unstoppable Power of Leaderless Organizations.* New York: Portfolio, 2006.

Harari, Yuval Noah. *Homo Deus: A Brief History of Tomorrow.* London: Vintage, 2016.

Heffernan, Margaret. *Uncharted: How to Navigate the Future.* London: Simon & Schuster UK, 2020.

Ismail, Salim. *Exponential Organizations: Why New Organizations Are Ten Times Better, Faster, and Cheaper Than Yours (and What to Do About It).* New York: Diversion Books, 2014.

Knight, Reid. *Hacking Leadership: The 11 Gaps Every Business Needs to Close and the Secrets to Closing Them Quickly.* Hoboken: Wiley, 2014.

Laloux, Frederic. *Reinventing Organizations: A Guide to Creating Organizations Inspired by the Next Stage of Human Consciousness.* Brussels: Nelson Parker, 2014.

Raworth, Kate. *Doughnut Economics: Seven Ways to Think Like a 21st-Century Economist.* London: Random House Business, 2017.

Ries, Eric. *The Lean Startup: How Today's Entrepreneurs Use Continuous Innovation to Create Radically Successful Businesses.* New York: Crown Business, 2011.

Uhl-Bien, Mary, and Russ Marion. *Complexity Leadership: Part 1: Conceptual Foundations.* Charlotte: Information Age Publishing, 2008.

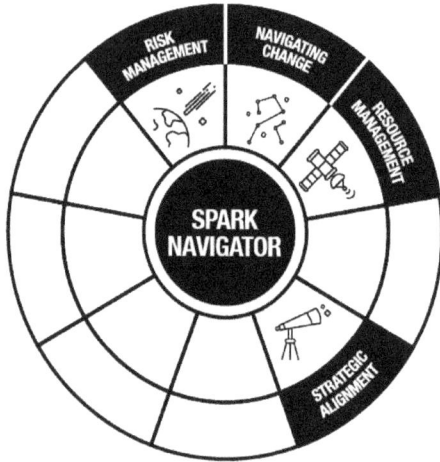

NAVIGATING CHANGE (CH)

RESOURCE MANAGEMENT (RE)

STRATEGIC ALIGNMENT (AL)

RISK MANAGEMENT (RI)

SPACE TO THINK

IN OUR relentless pursuit of actionable outcomes and tangible results, there lies a subtle yet profoundly powerful element that is too easily deprioritised or forgotten completely: the act of creating the space and environment to think.

This is about being present. In the moment. Giving the right attention to your thinking. Even in space, you need space to think...

In the sprawling cosmos of the Gemini Sector, aboard the flagship *Nexus*, Captain Elara faced a cacophony of urgent issues demanding her attention. The communications console was awash with alerts, each presenting seemingly critical problems from various departments of the ship. It was a classic scenario where the loudest voices often dominated strategic decisions. However, Captain Elara, a proponent of the strategic concept of 'space to think', decided to take a different approach.

Understanding the importance of clarity and focus in decision-making, Elara initiated a quiet period aboard the

Nexus. This was a deliberate strategy to temporarily distance the command crew from the barrage of pressing but potentially distracting issues. By creating this mental and physical space, she aimed to provide herself and her team with the opportunity to think clearly and deeply about the broader mission objectives, rather than reacting impulsively to immediate demands.

In this calmer environment, free from the constant noise of incoming communications, the team could reflect on their priorities with a clear mind. This approach allowed them to distinguish between genuinely critical issues requiring immediate action and those that were merely loud or urgent, but less important in the grand scheme of things.

Captain Elara's space-to-think approach proved to be transformative. In the newfound quiet, the team could discern that many of the urgent alerts were, in fact, minor or could be resolved with more measured responses. This period of reflection enabled the team to prioritise tasks more effectively, focusing on decisions that aligned with the *Nexus*'s long-term strategic goals and mission success.

By shifting focus from reacting to the loudest issues to contemplating the most impactful ones, Captain Elara and her team crafted a more thoughtful and efficient strategy. This approach not only resolved the immediate barrage of problems more effectively, but also paved the way for more proactive and calculated decision-making in the future.

Captain Elara's leadership in the Gemini Sector became a case study in strategic management, highlighting the importance of creating mental space to think clearly amid chaos. Her ability to filter out the noise and focus on what truly mattered ensured not just the success of the *Nexus*'s immediate mission, but also its sustained effectiveness in the longer term.

On Earth, drawing upon my experience across the for-purpose and nonprofit sectors, I've observed over and over again how transformative strategic decisions can teeter in the chaos of everyday life. How great ideas are malnourished because of a lack of time or attention.

Let's untangle this idea. At its essence, creating the 'space' isn't about carving out a physical or temporal niche. It's about fostering an environment that encourages deep contemplation, unburdened by the immediate pressures of 'doing something'. Yes... I can already hear you say, 'What time?!'

Good strategic thinking needs air to breathe.

It's a realm where thoughts are allowed to marinate, intermingle and evolve, giving birth to strategies that aren't just reactions but are well-considered responses. As the philosopher Bertrand Russell once remarked, 'The time you enjoy wasting is not wasted time.' This sentiment, while seemingly counterintuitive in our hustle-centric culture, captures the essence of our discourse.

When to use this Spark

This Spark is best used when confronted with challenges that seem perennial and issues that recur despite varied solutions. It's a cue to step back. Maybe also when you face monumental situations or ramifications... the bigger the issue, the bigger the space needed. You might need space when dealing with complex matters, resolving conflict, facing major change or trying to innovate. Phew, that's enough to make anyone feel burnt out—another time when space to think is critical.

The act of creating space to think is foundational. It ensures that subsequent tools are employed with clarity and purpose. It's the difference between using a compass and a map. While the map offers multiple routes, the compass ensures you're oriented correctly to begin with. As the edgy book *Deep Work* by Cal Newport posits, in an age of distraction, the ability to focus without distraction on a cognitively demanding task is becoming increasingly rare, and hence increasingly valuable.

How to use this Spark

There are two dimensions to giving something space. The first is about clearing away clutter and focusing on the matter at hand. The second is about purposefully pushing the matter into the subconscious processing part of your brain, letting your subconscious do some of the heavy lifting behind the scenes, and then returning to focus on it later.

I do both and often.

For me, this type of strategic thinking goes as follows:

1 Set aside clear, quiet and bounded time to initially focus on the matter (use some of the other Sparks during this allotted time).

2 At the end of the allotted time, diarise another time, about two days out, to revisit the matter.

3 Redeploy some of the other Sparks during this revisit (choose these based on the type of matter or problem) and brainstorm your response on your whiteboard.

4 Sense-check your thinking with others using the following two steps.

5 Send them material to review and ask them to read it a couple of days prior to seeking their thoughts.

6 Chat with them a few days later.

The outcomes of using this Spark

Utilising space-to-think in strategic thinking leads to a multitude of practical outcomes:

- **Enhanced decision-making:** In the throes of constant action, strategic thinking can become clouded. Providing space for contemplation leads to more thorough analysis, better risk assessment and more informed decisions.

- **Deeper understanding of complex issues:** Space to think enables you to dissect problems more thoroughly, uncovering root causes rather than just addressing symptoms.

- **Mental clarity:** The relentless pace of strategic leadership can be mentally taxing. Regularly scheduled thinking space is vital for mental health and sustained high performance. It can prevent burnout.

- **Better strategic alignment:** Actions and decisions consistently align with the broader vision and goals, maintaining strategic coherence. This is made possible because the space is made to assess that alignment.

- **Improved innovation:** Space to think provides room for creativity and innovation, essential for developing new ideas and approaches in response to evolving market demands.

- **Adaptability:** The opportunity exists to reassess and adjust strategies in light of new information or circumstances that may appear when given room.

- **Conflict resolution:** Space to think offers the necessary pause needed to approach conflicts or challenges thoughtfully, ensuring more effective resolution strategies.

Let the universe serve as a poignant reminder: the solutions to our most pressing challenges might be found not in the hustle and bustle, but in the silent, spacious moments where we grant ourselves the room to think, reimagine and strategise.

⚠ Dangers to beware of

When integrating space-to-think into your strategic approach, be mindful of potential challenges:

- **Procrastination:** While space is valuable, procrastination is a curse.

- **Isolation:** While creating space and pushing other things away for focus is beneficial, being too detached from the other things on your plate can lead to a disconnect from the practical realities and immediate needs of the organisation.

- **Carelessness:** It's a trap to push something out of mind, saying it needs space, and then only bringing it back into focus in a very cursory way. Be purposeful in creating the space and disciplined in frequently shining your light back on the subject.

- **Inconsistent application:** To be effective, space-to-think needs to be a regular and disciplined part of your routine and not just used sporadically.

- **Creating an echo chamber:** Be cautious of only reflecting within your own perspective. Seeking diverse viewpoints can enhance the value of your thinking space.

By being aware of these factors, you can effectively leverage space-to-think in your strategic planning, ensuring it serves as a tool for enhancement rather than being a hindrance.

🛠️ Capability-building tools & techniques

For those keen to embed this ethos within their organisational fabric, consider the following steps:

- **Dedicate time:** Institutionalise reflection periods. Whether it's a dedicated hour once a week or a strategic offsite once a month, ensure there's time earmarked for contemplation.

- **Create a conducive environment:** This isn't just about a physical space, but also about cultivating a culture where deep thinking is valued. Encourage your team to disconnect from digital distractions.

- **Promote diverse inputs:** Encourage team members to draw inspiration from varied sources—books, seminars, even nature walks. Different perspectives enrich strategic thought.

- **Document and revisit:** Ensure reflections are documented. Revisit them periodically, allowing ideas to evolve over time.

- **Act with purpose:** Post reflection, ensure there's a structured avenue to channel those insights into actionable strategies.

- **Iterate:** Reflect on your reflections. This meta-analysis ensures continuous improvement in the very way you think.

You will see that these tools are not just things to read or use; they are behaviours and cultural development techniques. This Spark calls for us to cross disciplinary boundaries and go beyond our logic.

CASE STUDY
NONPROFIT ORGANISATION FLOURISHES

Let's talk about the For-Purpose Foundation, a nonprofit that was perpetually in crisis mode. Grants to apply for, stakeholders to please, communities to serve—you name it. Knowing something had to change but not quite sure what, the foundation reached out to my firm.

What did we do? We implemented a mandatory, weekly space-to-think hour. These were sacred, non-negotiable pockets of time that employees spent away from their usual work. Now, you might be thinking, 'An hour a week? That's it?' But let me tell you, that hour worked like a charm. It empowered the team to step back and take a 10,000-foot view. It became a crucible for aligning their actions with the broader strategy of the organisation.

The result? Remarkable. Productivity surged, not because they were doing more, but because they were doing what mattered. Their grant success rate increased by thirty per cent, and employee turnover plummeted. They discovered innovative solutions to chronic problems that were sapping their resources. Like the proverbial pause that refreshes, this practice acted as a system reboot for the organisation, giving it the clarity it desperately needed.

Resources and references

Here are some references for you to deep dive (into deep space):

Harari, Yuval Noah. *21 Lessons for the 21st Century*. London: Spiegel & Grau, 2018.

Ito, Joi, and Jeff Howe. *Whiplash: How to Survive Our Faster Future*. New York: Grand Central Publishing, 2016.

Klein, Naomi. *This Changes Everything: Capitalism vs. the Climate*. New York: Simon & Schuster, 2014.

Newport, Cal. *Deep Work: Rules for Focused Success in a Distracted World*. New York: Grand Central Publishing, 2016.

O'Neil, Cathy. *Weapons of Math Destruction: How Big Data Increases Inequality and Threatens Democracy*. New York: Crown, 2016.

Raskino, Mark, and Graham Waller. *Digital to the Core: Remastering Leadership for Your Industry, Your Enterprise, and Yourself*. Stamford: Gartner, Inc., 2015.

Scott, Kim. Radical Candor: *Be a Kick-Ass Boss Without Losing Your Humanity*. New York: St. Martin's Press, 2017.

Taleb, Nassim Nicholas. *Skin in the Game: Hidden Asymmetries in Daily Life*. New York: Random House, 2018.

Zuberi, Daniyal. *Precarious Lives: Job Insecurity and Well-Being in Rich Democracies*. Cambridge: Polity, 2018.

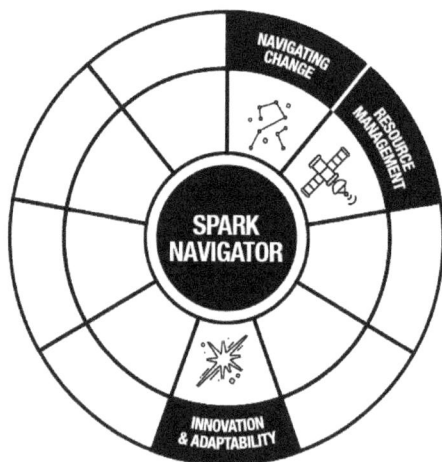

NAVIGATING CHANGE (CH)

RESOURCE MANAGEMENT (RE)

INNOVATION & ADAPTABILITY (IN)

COLLABORATIVE INTELLIGENCE H+AI

COLLABORATIVE INTELLIGENCE has two heartbeats: the human (H) and the machine (AI). Human + machine intelligence = H+AI. H+AI goes beyond the confines of simple teamwork, involving a blend of human intuition and machine capabilities. Woven together, in the right circumstances, human and machine intelligence produce thinking better than you or I could ever do alone…

In the complex network of the Centauri Star System, the AI-enhanced command ship, the *Pegasus*, was out of control during the longest hyperspace jump it had attempted. Captain Vega had the Comm. Vega and her team were at a loss to explain why this was happening and how long they had before the ship was torn apart. The only thing they did know was that if they shut down power to half of the ship, they could boost the engines and potentially regain navigational control.

Vega was known for her adept strategic thinking, and she realised the situation called for collaborative intelligence—a synergy of human insight and AI's analytical prowess. She initiated a 'crash' session with her crew and the ship's advanced AI, Artemis. Artemis brought unparalleled data processing capabilities, analysing vast streams of information and generating multiple strategic scenarios at incredible speeds. Meanwhile, the human crew members contributed contextual understanding, ethical considerations and creative problem-solving skills that Artemis couldn't replicate.

Together, they examined the issue from all angles, with Artemis providing real-time data analysis and predictive modelling, while the crew injected elements of human experience, intuition and values-based judgement. This synergy led to the development of a strategy that was both data-driven and human-centric, leveraging the strengths of both human and AI.

The implementation of this collaborative intelligence strategy proved highly effective; the crew regained control of the *Pegasus* while setting a new standard for decision-making in the Centauri Star System.

Captain Vega's approach highlighted the power of combining human and artificial intelligence, emphasising that the future of strategic thinking lies not in choosing between human and AI capabilities, but in harmonising them for greater insight, innovation and impact.

By interweaving artificial intelligence, big data and human insight, H+AI offers an enhanced problem-solving capacity that neither machines nor humans can achieve individually. It's like a symphony of cognitive diversity, where each individual—or machine—plays a unique part but aims for a unified, harmonious outcome. The key here is 'integration', and it fundamentally changes how we approach strategic challenges, transforming our organisations into learning ecosystems.

When to use this Spark

H+AI is ideal in complex data analysis situations, where AI can process vast amounts of information, providing insights for human strategists to interpret and build upon. It's valuable in predictive modelling, where AI's ability to identify patterns and trends complements human foresight and experience. It's also crucial in decision-making processes involving large datasets, where AI can quickly provide options and humans can apply contextual understanding and ethical considerations. Furthermore, you should employ H+AI in innovation, where AI-generated possibilities can be refined and directed by human creativity and market understanding.

H+AI is evolving more quickly than human intelligence and while today it is best used in research, bulk analysis and synthesis, it won't be this limited for much longer.

How to use this Spark

Here is an introductory method that I often use with this Spark:

1   **Rally the humans:** Get the right minds into the room and work together to agree on the right question! Then agree on what information and data is needed to answer this question. Finally, ask the collective mind to develop a hypothesis solution to start with.

2   **Gather data with AI:** Use AI tools to do research, and to gather and analyse data. For instance, AI can go beyond databases and find articles, sift through social media and locate big datasets.

3   Ask the AI for a hypothesis and strategies to address.

4   **Re-inject human analysis and interpretation:** The strategy team reviews the AI-generated data. They bring their industry knowledge, understanding of company values and experience to interpret this data.

5   **Scenario planning:** Combine AI's predictive models with team brainstorming to explore expansion strategies. AI can simulate various scenarios based on the identified trend, while the team contributes creative ideas and considers practical implications.

6   **Decision-making:** Use both AI insights and human judgement to decide on the best course of action.

7   **Implementation and feedback loop:** Implement the strategy and use AI to monitor its effectiveness, adjusting based on real-time data and team evaluations.

☑ The outcomes of using this Spark

Collaborative intelligence, blending multiple humans' insights with AI's computational power, stands out in strategic thinking for several compelling reasons:

- **Thinking efficiency:** Collaborative intelligence leads to more precise predictions and informed decisions. AI handles complex data analysis rapidly, freeing human strategists to focus on strategic interpretation and application, thus accelerating the planning and execution process. With AI handling the heavy lifting of data processing, human strategists can focus on strategic interpretation and decision-making.

- **More comprehensive analysis:** AI has the ability to process vast datasets and identify patterns at an unprecedented scale. Using a collaborative approach adds the nuanced, contextual and ethical understanding of human intelligence. This synergy between human and machine leads to richer insights and more informed decisions.

- **Expanded innovation options:** The combination of human creativity with AI's analytical capabilities harnesses the best of both worlds. It facilitates innovative solutions by combining human creativity with AI's predictive modelling capabilities, thus expanding the scope of traditional strategic thinking.

- **Robust risk management:** The predictive strength of AI, coupled with human judgement, also creates a powerful framework for early identification and mitigation of risks.

AI is making its presence felt in our brave new world, but it cannot do the kind of thinking you can do. When we add human intelligence and collaborate with AI, the benefits become exponential.

⚠ Dangers to beware of

When employing collaborative intelligence in strategic thinking, be mindful of these considerations:

- **Over-reliance on AI:** Avoid relying solely on AI. It's crucial to maintain a balance between AI insights and human judgement.

- **Poor data quality and bias:** Ensure the data fed into AI systems is high quality and free from biases, as flawed data can lead to inaccurate outcomes.

- **Misinterpretation of AI outputs:** Be cautious in interpreting AI-generated insights. They need to be contextualised and understood within the broader strategic framework.

- **Integration challenges:** Seamlessly integrating AI into strategic processes can be complex. Effective collaboration between AI and human intelligence requires careful planning and execution.

- **Failure to stay up to date with AI advancements:** AI is advancing rapidly. Make sure you stay updated with advancements in AI to fully leverage its capabilities in strategic thinking.

- **Unethical practices:** Be aware of ethical implications, especially around data privacy and AI transparency, to maintain trust and integrity in your strategies.

By being aware of these potential challenges, you can more effectively harness the power of collaborative intelligence in strategic thinking.

🛠 Capability-building tools & techniques

Here are some ways to build this Spark muscle:

- **Continuous learning in AI trends:** Stay abreast of the latest developments in AI technology and applications. Engaging with current research, attending relevant webinars and subscribing to tech journals can keep you informed.

- **AI workshops and training:** Enrol in workshops or online courses focusing on AI and its strategic applications. This hands-on experience will deepen your understanding of AI capabilities.

- **Collaboration with AI experts:** Establish connections with AI professionals. Their insights can provide practical perspectives on integrating AI into strategic planning effectively.

- **AI-powered analytics tools:** Regularly use AI-driven data analysis tools in your strategic planning. Familiarity with these tools will enhance your ability to interpret and utilise AI-generated insights.

- **Critical thinking and interpretation skills:** Strengthen your critical thinking abilities to effectively interpret AI data and insights within the context of your strategic objectives.

- **Simulated strategic scenarios:** Engage in simulated exercises that combine AI data with strategic decision-making. This practice can enhance your ability to integrate AI insights into real-world scenarios.

By adopting these methods, you'll not only deepen your understanding of AI's role in strategic thinking, but also refine your ability to synergise AI capabilities with your strategic acumen.

CASE STUDY
FOODFORWARD FOUNDATION

Collaborative intelligence isn't just a buzzword; it's a transformative tool that can genuinely drive impact, as demonstrated by the FoodForward Foundation. The foundation was grappling with food insecurity, a multifaceted issue that was both profoundly driven by system failures and overflowing with plentiful datasets. It needed an insightful approach. And that's exactly where collaborative intelligence came into play.

The foundation gathered a group of experts—from farmers to supply chain experts, from nutritionists to community leaders—to help it identify the system break points. This group also captured the value propositions for each stakeholder in each part of the system.

This work led to the development of 'a design and a set of design principles' for a new, more efficient and human-centric system that engaged everyone. But this design needed to be tested to see if it could and would actually work. Data (such as supply chain data, consumption data, wastage data, and so on) was plentiful, but came in a variety of sources and formats. It was slow going to manually sort through this data lake. This is where AI shone.

The team were able to harness the power of AI to crunch through, sort and develop insights from the sea of data. With these insights, scenarios could be developed and again AI was able to step in to help run these scenarios against the data.

The result was a food distribution system that was not only more efficient, but also significantly more sustainable. Farmers supplied fresh enough produce and reduced waste, while supply chain experts implemented a last-mile delivery model to ensure food reached the communities and people most at risk. Nutritionists formulated balanced meal plans, and community leaders executed the distribution. The result was a forty-five per cent increase in the reach of food distribution and a twenty per cent decrease in food wastage within the first year.

But let's not forget the most compelling statistic: a thirty per cent increase in community engagement. Why? Because everyone felt they had a stake in solving the problem. This is the power of collaborative intelligence. It's not just a way to solve complex problems; it's a strategy for engaging everyone in the solution.

📖 Resources and references

These sources offer a wide range of perspectives, from the integration of artificial intelligence in team settings to the influence of gender and diversity on collective intelligence. It's a robust list that should offer profound insights into the complex but rewarding world of collaborative intelligence:

Frick, Walter. 'Artificial Intelligence Needs a Strong Human
    Element'. *Harvard Business Review*, 2018.

Kittur, Aniket, Jeffrey V. Nickerson, Michael S. Bernstein. 'The
    Future of Crowd Work'. *ACM*, 2013.

Malhotra, Deepak, and Michael A. Hogg. 'The Dynamics of
    Collaborative Intelligence: Exploring Human and Machine
    Networks in Complex Problem Solving'. *Harvard Business
    Review*, 2020.

Muralidharan, Anand, and Hyunjin Kim. 'Collaborative
    Intelligence: When Humans and Machines Work
    Together'. *Journal of Artificial Intelligence*, 2020.

Mulgan, Geoff. *Collective Intelligence: An Introduction.* Palgrave
    Macmillan, 2018.

Page, Scott E. *The Diversity Bonus: How Great Teams Pay Off in
    the Knowledge Economy.* Princeton University Press, 2019.

Reeves, Martin, and Daichi Ueda. 'The Power of Collective
    Intelligence'. *Boston Consulting Group*, 2020.

Rock, David, and Heidi Grant. 'Why Diverse Teams Are
    Smarter'. *Harvard Business Review*, 2016.

Wilson, H. James, and Paul R. Daugherty. 'Collaborative
    Intelligence: Humans and AI Are Joining Forces'. *Harvard
    Business Review*, 2018.

Woolley, Anita Williams, and Thomas W. Malone. 'Defend
    Your Research: What Makes a Team Smarter? More
    Women'. *Harvard Business Review*, 2011.

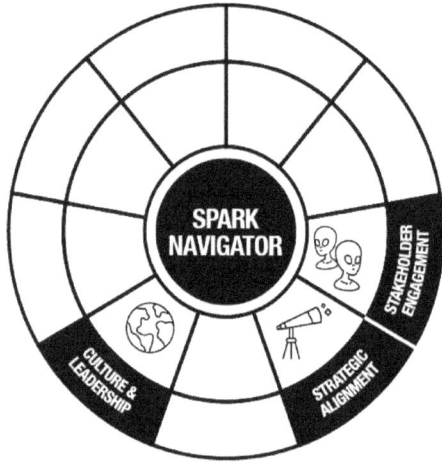

STAKEHOLDER ENGAGEMENT (ST)

STRATEGIC ALIGNMENT (AL)

CULTURE & LEADERSHIP (CL)

TRIUNE BRAINS

THERE IS a fascinating model of the human brain called the 'triune brain', which was proposed by American physician and neuroscientist Paul D. Mac-Lean. It postulates that your brain is a composite of three distinct brains developed through your evolutionary journey: the reptilian complex (base instincts), the limbic system (emotions) and the neo-cortex (rational thinking).

When you peer into the vast expanse of space, you're not merely looking at stars and galaxies. You're observing a realm that requires an intricate dance of logic, emotion and instinct to truly understand and appreciate—a dance that mirrors your brain's functions.

Picture this: an organisation is much like a spaceship, venturing into the unknown, aiming for a distant star. The oldest part of your brain—the 'reptilian brain'—is the ship's engine, driving forward, seeking sustenance and survival. It ensures that the ship avoids meteor showers and black holes by reacting swiftly to immediate threats.

Then, there's the limbic system—the emotional cen-tre—which is akin to the crew members aboard the ship. They bring the human element, the camaraderie and the spirit, ensuring that the journey is not just about survival, but also about experiencing joy, wonder and connection.

Lastly, the ship's state-of-the-art navigation system represents the neocortex, processing vast amounts of data, planning the route and strategising for potential challenges. It's this part that ponders the greater ques-tions: Why are we heading to this star? What do we hope to achieve?

The description of the human brain I have just compared to space travel—the triune brain—while sometimes contested in the academic field, offers a profound perspective on human decision-making, pivotal for strategic thinkers.

I am a person who believes in more than logic and that we process things with more than just our brains, so this model appeals to me.

This thinking was further developed in recent years, with other academics conducting research into the body as a processing structure (that is, illness and disease as expressions of emotions and trauma). Here, I am focusing on Paul D. MacLean's idea: 'To understand the imbalances of our modern world, we must recognise the evolutionary imbalances of our brain.'

When one strategises, one must be conscious of which 'brain' is in the driver's seat.

The reptilian brain seeks to meet your basic needs and keep you safe—is your thinking driven by these needs and is that appropriate?

The limbic system highlights the role of emotional intelligence and seeks to address things like the impact of morale on team performance. Are you shaping strategies with too much or not enough consideration of people in the mix?

Lastly, the neocortex represents the analytical and critical thinking essential for complex problem-solving and innovation. Are you overplaying this logical approach at the expense of other forms of thinking?

Are you acting out of primal instinct, emotional impulse or rational analysis? Often, the most effective strategies are formulated when we can harmoniously integrate all three, considering our base instincts, emotional intelligence and analytical prowess.

When to use this Spark

Ideally use this Spark as a checklist through the hypothesis, concept and implementation stages of each project.

In comparison to other strategic concepts, the triune brain offers unparalleled insight into the human condition. While other theories may analyse the 'what' and 'how' of strategic outcomes, the triune brain delves into the 'why'. A great time to use this Spark is when your logic is feeling stuck and your intuition is telling you to press on.

How to use this Spark

I tend to deploy this Spark as a checklist when I'm working through a project or matter, and apply it at key concept stages in the work. I didn't always, and that led to elegant strategies that fell flat. The checklist goes like this:

1   **Address reptilian brain needs:** Assess that the thinking explicitly addresses organisational stability and safety. Establish clear structures and protocols that provide this sense of security.

2   **Engage the limbic system:** Focus on emotional intelligence within your thinking, hypothesis and solutions. Acknowledge the ability of emotions to enhance or derail the strategy. This step is crucial for maintaining high morale and motivation, which are essential for effective collaboration and stakeholder engagement.

3   **Leverage the neocortex:** Stress-test whether you are using enough critical and analytical skills in your thinking. This involves not only data analysis, but also long-term visioning and innovative problem-solving.

By systematically addressing each layer of the triune brain, you create strategies that are secure and stable, emotionally resonant and intellectually sound, ensuring a well-rounded and effective approach to any strategic challenge.

☑ The outcomes of using this Spark

The outcomes derived from applying the triune brain concept in strategic thinking are multifold. It promotes a holistic understanding of decision-making drivers, equipping the strategist to anticipate reactions better and craft strategies that resonate more deeply with their intended audience. It's not just about understanding facts and figures; it's about understanding people.

Utilising the triune brain model in strategic thinking leads to many positive outcomes, including:

- **Stability:** Honouring the considerations of the reptile brain ensures stakeholders are not destabilised by the strategy.

- **Enhanced team morale:** Engaging through emotional intelligence—that is, tapping into the limbic system—during strategic thinking fosters better teamwork and a positive attitude towards the strategy.

- **Stronger stakeholder relationships:** Emotional intelligence helps in building and maintaining robust stakeholder connections to the strategy.

- **Increased creativity and innovation:** A secure and emotionally intelligent environment nurtures creativity and new ideas in your team's strategic thinking.

- **Improved decision- and design-making:** Leveraging the neocortex aids in logical, informed and innovative decision- and design-making processes.

- **Adaptability:** Balancing all brain functions enhances organisational flexibility and adaptability to change.

This approach ensures strategic plans are comprehensive, resilient and attuned to both human and organisational needs.

⚠ Dangers to beware of

When applying the triune brain model in strategic thinking, be mindful of the following:

- **Overemphasis on one aspect:** Avoid focusing too heavily on one brain layer at the expense of others. Balancing the reptilian, limbic and neocortex functions is crucial for a well-rounded strategy.

- **Misinterpreting emotional responses:** While engaging the limbic system, be cautious not to misinterpret or oversimplify emotional responses. Emotional intelligence requires nuanced understanding and sensitivity to flow through into your strategic design.

- **Neglecting individual differences:** People respond differently based on their unique brain functioning. Be aware of these differences in your team and adapt your approach to thinking accordingly.

- **Underestimating the complexity of interactions:** The interplay between the brain's three layers can be complex. Be prepared for unexpected interactions and outcomes when addressing each layer, especially when helping others think this way—being so explicit is often new and can frustrate those who like to 'leap' to solutions.

- **Ignoring external factors:** This Spark is inherently internally focused. Don't overlook external environmental factors that can significantly impact your strategic thinking.

- **Rigid application of the model:** The triune brain model is a framework, not a strict rule. Stay flexible in its application and open to insights that may not fit neatly within this model.

Being aware of these potential challenges will help you effectively leverage the triune brain model in strategic planning, ensuring a balanced and adaptable approach.

⚒ Capability-building tools & techniques

For those keen to embed this knowledge into their strategic arsenal, several psychological tools and practices can be instrumental:

- **Neurofeedback training:** Originally used to treat conditions like ADHD, this technology can provide real-time data about brain activity. By understanding and witnessing how different parts of the brain activate under various stimuli, one can tailor strategies to appeal to those specific areas.

- **Immersive role-playing:** Role-playing games, especially in virtual reality, can offer experiential insight into different decision-making processes. By placing oneself in various scenarios, you can observe which parts of the brain you naturally tap into and which you might be neglecting.

- **Sensory deprivation tanks:** These tanks, also known as float tanks, deprive you of sensory input, forcing different parts of your brain to become more active. It's a meditative experience that can heighten awareness of your primal instincts and emotions.

- **Interactive workshops with actors:** Employ professional actors to enact scenarios based on primal instincts, emotional responses and rational deliberations. This can vividly illustrate the triune brain's reactions in real-time, providing deeper insights.

- **Experimental decision-making retreats:** Attend or create retreats where participants make decisions under various conditions—extreme stress, emotional duress or using pure logic puzzles. This helps illuminate which part of the triune brain is dominant and under what circumstances.

- **Neurological apps:** Apps like Brainwell or Peak offer games designed around neuroscientific principles. These can sharpen specific parts of the brain, making you more attuned to how each part responds to different stimuli.

Remember, while these tools can offer deeper insights into the workings of the triune brain, it's essential to approach them with an open mind and a pinch of scepticism. What works profoundly for one might not resonate as deeply with another. Always seek to balance experiential learning with foundational knowledge.

⊖ CASE STUDY
BEYOND OUR STREETS—
A NONPROFIT TRIUMPH

In Melbourne, the nonprofit Beyond Our Streets embarked on an ambitious project. Its goal? Tackle homelessness by tapping into the very psyche of society. It turned to the triune brain model to develop its strategies, realising that to evoke change, it needed to resonate on instinctual, emotional and rational levels.

At the heart of its campaign was a series of powerful visuals. A reptilian brain responds to stark, clear, visual cues—the stuff of basic survival. So, it showcased images of dilapidated buildings juxtaposed with potential refurbished shelters. This viscerally conveyed the 'threat' of homelessness and the 'safety' of shelter.

Simultaneously, it launched emotionally charged storytelling sessions where the homeless shared their heart-wrenching journeys. These stories connected with the public at an emotional, limbic level, fostering empathy and humanising the faceless statistics of homelessness.

Lastly, with the neocortex—the rational brain—in mind, it developed workshops and published comprehensive literature on the societal cost of homelessness and the economic benefits of its proposed solutions.

By the year's end, Beyond Our Streets had not only exceeded its fundraising target, but had also spurred local businesses and communities into action. It tapped into our primal, emotional and rational drives, crafting a strategy that was holistically human.

📖 Resources and references

To deepen your understanding, here are some further resources.

Sagan, Carl. *The Dragons of Eden: Speculations on the Evolution of Human Intelligence*. New York: Random House, 1977.

NeuroStrategy.com. https://www.igi-global.com/dictionary/neurostrategy/91955

MacLean, Paul D. *Triune Brain in Evolution*. Springer, 1990.

The Marginalian, www.themarginalian.org

Your Triune Brain. YouTube documentary series.

The Brains Blog www.philosophyofbrains.com See section on evolutionary psychology.

The Reptilian Brain Podcast.

EQInstitute.org. www.eqinst.org

Carlson, D. John. 'Use Your Neocortex to Develop Strategy'. https://www.linkedin.com/pulse/use-your-neo-cortex-develop-strategy-d-john-carlson/

RESOURCE MANAGEMENT (RE)

STAKEHOLDER ENGAGEMENT (ST)

CULTURE & LEADERSHIP (CL)

GETTING PAST YOURSELF

THE CHALLENGE of getting past yourself, as I've come to appreciate deeply over my years of facilitating and developing strategy, is about your inherent ability (or inability) to transcend your own biases, perceptions and deeply ingrained beliefs to create strategies that genuinely resonate with changing landscapes and diverse perspectives.

This is hard. Especially when your 'gut' tells you the answer is right in front of you and you should push past to the next problem to solve!

Consider the early days of space exploration. Scientists and astronomers, deeply entrenched in their convictions, were focused on close celestial bodies like the Moon or Mars. It was the known, the familiar.

However, Dr Eleanor Hartfield, a pioneering astrophysicist from Melbourne, challenged this limited perspective. She believed that the answers to the universe's mysteries lay not just in our immediate cosmic neighbourhood, but in the uncharted depths of space beyond our galaxy. Dr Hartfield championed the idea of 'getting past ourselves' to the global astronomy community. Rather than being tethered to prevailing notions, she advocated for exploring the unexplored, delving into deep space, and pushing the boundaries of our cosmic knowledge.

Inspired by her perspective, global space agencies began investing in telescopes capable of peering into the most distant reaches of space, leading to groundbreaking discoveries about dark matter, black holes and even potential life-bearing exoplanets.

Dr Hartfield's cosmic journey underscores the essence of this Spark. To truly innovate and discover, whether in strategy or space exploration, you must first transcend your inherent biases and dare to venture where few have gone before.

Getting past yourself embodies the essence of self-awareness and the constant quest for personal growth in the strategic realm. As the iconic Australian strategist Lawrence Kennedy once observed, 'In strategy, as in life, our greatest enemy is often the limitations we place upon ourselves.' Truer words have seldom been spoken. To truly lead, innovate and shape the future, you must first confront and overcome your self-imposed boundaries.

When to use this Spark

There are scenarios in which pushing past personal limitations enables a more dynamic, flexible approach to strategy, essential for navigating complex, unfamiliar or rapidly changing environments. These include innovation deadlocks and strategic pivots, when managing a crisis or instigating diversity and inclusion initiatives. This Spark is also particularly effective when engaging in collaborative ventures.

Getting past yourself in strategic thinking is superior in these cases because it fosters a more open, innovative and adaptable approach, crucial for success in an increasingly complex and dynamic business landscape.

How to use this Spark

Getting past your own limitations in strategic thinking involves a series of deliberate steps:

1 **Develop self-awareness:** Begin by identifying your own biases and limitations, especially in regard to the topic you want to think strategically about. Reflect on past decisions and consider feedback from diverse sources to understand your habitual patterns and blind spots.

2 **Get out of your echo chamber:** Actively engage with people from different backgrounds or disciplines on both the topic and your initial thinking. This can involve consulting with team members who bring unique viewpoints or seeking insights from external stakeholders and experts.

3 **Swallow the feedback:** Your thinking alone is probably not always enough. Push yourself to openly take on feedback. View criticism as

opportunities to develop your thinking rather than insurmountable obstacles. Emphasise the value of learning over the fear of being seen to be wrong.

4   **Encourage open feedback:** Share the feedback you have received to create an environment where constructive criticism is welcomed and valued.

5   **Experimentation:** Embark on trial and error using your thinking and the feedback to develop your strategic approaches.

6   **Surrender to collaborative problem-solving:** Engage in, and even step back and watch, brainstorming sessions and collaborative workshops on your thinking. Encourage team members to contribute ideas and solutions, fostering a culture of collaborative intelligence.

7   **Reflect and adjust:** Regularly review your strategies and approaches. Reflect on what's working and what's not, and be prepared to pivot or adjust your plans based on these insights.

By following these steps, you can effectively move beyond personal limitations, leveraging a more comprehensive and diverse approach to strategic thinking. This not only broadens your perspective, but also enhances the overall quality and effectiveness of your strategic decisions.

☑ The outcomes of using this Spark

What are the benefits of using this Spark? I believe you can expect the following outcomes:

- **Enhanced strategic visioning:** Getting past yourself encourages thinking beyond the current paradigm, allowing for long-term, visionary planning that anticipates future trends and disruptions.

- **Personal development:** Constantly challenging one's own strategic assumptions fosters personal growth in strategic skills and insights.

- **Thinking resilience:** This Spark promotes the ability to meta-think; that is, to think about your thinking. Psychologists call this metacognition. Such meta thinking will see you assess, review and refine your thinking—all ways to build its resilience.

- **Richer scenario development:** You will seek a broader range of potential scenarios and outcomes to consider, enhancing the robustness of strategic thinking.

- **Diverse strategic inputs:** Actively seeking varied viewpoints leads to strategies that are more considerate of different market segments and stakeholder groups.

⚠ Dangers to beware of

In applying this Spark to your strategic thinking, you must make sure you don't fall into these nasty traps:

- **Rocking the boat:** While striving to push beyond conventional limits, it's essential to remain grounded in what's realistically achievable, ensuring that ambition doesn't overshadow practicality.

- **Assuming old means broken:** As much as I value innovation as a way to push past individual boundaries, I recognise the value that time-tested strategies can have. It's about finding that sweet spot between the novel and the reliable.

- **Analysis paralysis:** It's way too easy to go full tilt the other way and want to do too much preparation. Be cautious not to fall into a cycle of overthinking.

- **Losing touch with your core:** Some of those boundaries and biases you have are there for a good reason. It's crucial to ensure that these explorations don't lead you away from the fundamental principles and values that define you and your strategic approach.

Being aware of these points will help you apply this approach effectively, enhancing your strategic thinking without losing sight of your unique perspective and goals.

✂ Capability-building tools & techniques

Let's get practical now. What techniques can you use to implement this concept in your thinking?

- **Cognitive reframing:** This involves changing the way you view a situation to alter its emotional impact and your response to it. If you consistently view certain strategic challenges with trepidation due to past failures, cognitive reframing can help shift your perspective to see them as learning opportunities. Regularly challenge yourself: 'Is there another way to interpret this situation?'

- **Mindfulness and meditation:** These practices ground you in the present moment, helping to clear the clutter of past experiences or future anxieties. By practising mindfulness, you enhance your awareness of your immediate reactions and inherent biases. Even a daily ten-minute meditation practice can offer clarity, especially before making strategic decisions.

- **Counterfactual thinking:** This involves imagining alternative outcomes to events that have already occurred. For instance, if a past strategic initiative failed, instead of just focusing on what went wrong, think about the scenarios where it could have succeeded. What would have changed? This tool broadens your horizon, making you consider alternatives you might otherwise overlook.

- **Descriptive feedback sessions:** Instead of just seeking feedback, structure sessions where peers or mentors provide descriptive feedback. Rather than stating what was good or bad, they describe your actions and their observed outcomes. This offers a clearer mirror to your behaviours, aiding in self-awareness and identifying where personal biases might be influencing decisions.

- **Socratic questioning:** Named after the classical Greek philosopher Socrates, this method involves asking a series of open-ended questions to stimulate critical thinking. When faced with a strategic challenge, instead of jumping to solutions, pose a series of 'why', 'how' and 'what if' questions. This introspective enquiry can unearth biases and provide a more objective viewpoint. This is my personal favourite ... give it a try and be totally open to the answers others give you.

Applying these tools requires consistent practise. But, as I've observed across numerous boardrooms and strategy sessions, the benefits they bring in terms of clarity, objectivity and innovative thinking are profound. The landscape of strategy, especially in sectors like the for-purpose domain, is ever-evolving. The ability to continually refine one's thinking, breaking free from personal shackles, remains one of the most invaluable assets a strategist can possess.

CASE STUDY
RISEABOVE FOUNDATION'S TRANSFORMATION

Within the nonprofit sector, the tale of RiseAbove Foundation, a Melbourne-based organisation focused on youth development, serves as a compelling testament to the transformative power of getting past yourself.

For years, RiseAbove had been implementing a tried-and-tested model: physical workshops aimed at empowering young individuals. Yet, despite its best intentions, engagement numbers began dwindling. While easy to attribute this decline to external factors, the foundation's dynamic CEO, James Henderson, championed a different approach. At an annual strategy retreat, James introduced the concept of getting past yourself. It was time, he argued, for the organisation to challenge its deeply held beliefs and preconceptions about youth engagement.

In a bold move, RiseAbove pivoted away from its traditional workshop model. Recognising the digital-first nature of its target demographic, it embraced online platforms. Through a series of virtual engagement initiatives, including webinars, digital mentorship programs and interactive e-learning modules, it reconnected with its audience.

The results were profound. Engagement metrics soared, but, more importantly, feedback from the youth community highlighted a renewed sense of connection and empowerment. RiseAbove's story underscores a belief

I've long held: true strategic innovation often necessitates looking beyond your pre-existing beliefs and daring to forge a new path.

📖 Resources and references

Here are some resources to dive into to learn more about this Spark:

Carr, Isabelle. *Beyond the Self: Modern Strategic Thinking.* Melbourne: StrategyPress, 2020.

Chen, Felix. *The Power of Perspective in Strategy.* Brisbane: ThinkAhead Publications, 2022.

Gomez, Isabella. *Adaptive Strategies for Modern Times.* Adelaide: South Insights Publishing, 2021.

Green, Liam. 'Nonprofits and the Art of Self-Transcendence'. *Australian Strategy Quarterly*, 2022.

Howard, Clara. 'Corporates and Self-Transcendence: The Telstra Tale'. *Business Strategy Review*, 2021.

Mitchell, Aaron. *Thinking Past Limits.* Perth: Strategic Minds Publishing, 2019.

Patel, Nayan. *Government Innovations: The NSW Transport Revolution.* Sydney: Public Insights Publishing, 2021.

Rodriguez, Emilia. 'Strategy Without Borders'. *Strategic Innovations Journal*, 2020.

Ryan, Luke. 'Strategy Beyond Self'. *Corporate Strategies Today*, 2023.

Walker, Sophia. 'Unleashing Potential: Overcoming Self in Strategic Planning'. *Strategic Horizons*, 2020.

NAVIGATING CHANGE (CH)

INNOVATION & ADAPTABILITY (IN)

FINANCIAL STABILITY (FS)

RISK MANAGEMENT (RI)

VEIL OF RATIONALITY

IN REALITY, there is a veil clouding your judgement, concealing important factors like intuition, creativity and emotional intelligence, which are crucial in strategic thinking. Don't misunderstand me: data and logic are important, but they aren't the be-all and end-all. As Albert Einstein said, 'The intuitive mind is a sacred gift and the rational mind is a faithful servant. We have created a society that honours the servant and has forgotten the gift.'

Imagine this: when planning a mission to a distant planet, the planning team begins by collecting empirical data. This data includes details about orbital mechanics, fuel requirements and life-support systems. This information is critical to the mission; without it, it will be physically impossible to reach the target galaxy. And it would be easy to stop at the point where success seems assured. But the team planning this mission want to do more than simply hit a physical target—they want to lift the veil of rationality and consider the softer factors that will make the mission both a physical and human success.

When planning the mission, the team combine the rational and scientific data with intuitive insights from experienced astronauts about human endurance and adaptability in space. They also consider the emotional and psychological impacts of long-duration space travel. This blend of hard science with human factors leads to a mission plan that is not only technically sound but also attuned to the well-being of the crew, enhancing the mission's overall success and sustainability in the unforgiving environment of space.

In the Western world, rationalist and science-centric meta frameworks often favour and reward thinking and decisions that are based purely on logic and reason. This veil of rationality is a real problem. I believe it's one of the places where strategic thinking falls well short of realising its true potential.

Here's the kicker: it takes a keen self-awareness to even recognise you're operating under this veil. Like Plato's allegory of the cave, we often don't see the shadows for what they are—merely representations of a greater reality outside the cave. It's essential to challenge your assumptions continuously and question whether your so-called 'rational decisions' are as impartial as they seem. It's an introspective process, but an invaluable one.

The veil of rationality is not a nemesis to be vanquished, but a bias to be understood and balanced.

Sometimes, letting a bit of 'irrationality' in might make your strategy not just good, but extraordinary. So, the next time you find yourself saying, 'It's just common sense,' stop and think. Is it really? Or is it just the veil of rationality obscuring your vision? Lift it, and you might just find a whole new landscape of strategic possibilities.

When to use this Spark

So, when should you be on the lookout for this veil? When you're locked into a decision-making process and find yourself or your team over-relying on data. When there's a stubborn insistence that 'numbers don't lie.' When the conversation feels too linear, too cut-and-dry, and you start to think, 'Aren't we missing something here?' These are all good signs that the veil of rationality is at play.

The veil of rationality is best lifted in complex strategic situations where innovation, empathy or disruption are key. If you're planning a corporate takeover, by all means, keep the veil on and follow the numbers. But if you're looking to innovate, to pivot or to connect with stakeholders on an emotional level, then beware the constraints of the veil.

Lifting the veil of rationality embraces the full spectrum of human cognition, blending rational analysis with emotional and intuitive insights. It really works in today's complex world with its modern, global, strategic challenges, offering a more adaptive, inclusive and effective way of navigating the strategic landscape.

How to use this Spark

To effectively integrate this Spark into a strategic thinking process, I follow these specific, sequential steps:

1   **Prepare the ground:** At the outset, prepare yourself and your team for a different approach. Acknowledge upfront that your strategic thinking approach will consciously consider both rational analysis and emotional, intuitive inputs.

2   **Gather preliminary data:** Begin with traditional data collection and analysis. Look at the hard facts, figures and logical arguments pertinent to the strategy and draw your initial hypothesis and conclusions.

3   **Call out biases:** After analysing the data, hold a session to identify potential biases. Encourage team members to openly discuss and recognise biases that could influence their thinking and insights.

4   **Hang out the laundry:** Allocate a specific phase in the process for exploring emotional and intuitive insights. Ask team members to share gut feelings or emotional responses to the strategy and data presented and deep dive into why. Do not skip or shorten this step just because it's uncomfortable.

5 **Balance the discussion:** Facilitate a structured discussion to balance the rational data with the emotional and intuitive inputs. Explore how these different elements can complement each other in forming a comprehensive strategy.

6 **Incorporate diverse non-rational perspectives:** Actively seek the opinions and intuitions of various stakeholders, including led experience. This can include surveys, interviews or workshops with individuals who might be affected by or have insights into the strategy.

7 **Consolidate and synthesise:** Bring together the rational analysis, identified biases, emotional insights and diverse perspectives. Synthesise these elements to form a well-rounded strategic plan.

8 **Reflect and adjust:** Finally, reflect on this process. Evaluate the effectiveness of integrating both rational and emotional elements and make adjustments for future strategic planning.

By following these steps, you will ensure a thorough, inclusive approach to strategy that transcends the limitations of purely rational thinking.

☑ The outcomes of using this Spark

Employing the concept of lifting the veil of rationality in strategic thinking leads to several practical outcomes:

- **Better strategic thinking:** By integrating both logical and emotional insights, strategies become more nuanced and comprehensive.

- **Increased creativity:** This approach fosters a creative environment where unconventional ideas are explored, leading to innovative solutions.

- **Stronger team dynamics:** Encouraging a culture where both rational and emotional contributions are valued fosters a more inclusive and dynamic team environment.

- **Improved stakeholder engagement:** Lifting the veil of rationality creates ideas that resonate with stakeholders, enhancing their engagement and commitment to the strategy.

- **Greater adaptability:** This approach ensures flexibility and adaptability in strategic planning, crucial in a rapidly evolving business context.

- **Cognitive bias awareness:** Regularly challenging rational decisions with emotional and intuitive checks helps mitigate potential cognitive biases.

By embracing these outcomes, strategic thinking becomes more dynamic and aligned with the complex realities of modern decision-making environments.

⚠ Dangers to beware of

When employing this Spark in strategic thinking, watch out for these pitfalls:

- **Biases in disguise:** Be vigilant against letting biases masquerade as intuition. This can skew decisions.

- **Disregard of data:** Emotional insights should complement data, not replace it.

- **Subjectivity:** There's a fine line between intuition and subjectivity. Make sure you are aware of where that line is drawn.

- **Over-reliance on consensus:** While stakeholder buy-in is important, beware of striving for consensus at the expense of potentially more effective, albeit less popular, strategies.

- **Emotional overload:** Emotional inputs need to be managed carefully. It's all too easy to develop strategic 'darlings'—ideas you love. Killing these darlings can bring on significant veils or resistance, which will get in the way of good thinking.

- **Complexity in implementation:** Translating emotionally influenced strategies into actionable plans can be challenging.

- **Retrospective rationalisation:** It's all too easy to jump to a solution and rationalise it later. Ask yourself or your team mates to explain their rationality, rather than just accept it.

By being aware of these dangers, lifting the veil of rationality will lead to strategies that balance rational and intuitive thinking.

⚒ Capability-building tools & techniques

To anyone keen on navigating past this veil, here are some techniques to try:

- **Self-reflection:** Catch yourself. Are you oversimplifying? Are the metrics the whole story, or just a chapter?

- **Seeking diversity:** Engage with different voices. They can offer perspectives that pierce through the rationality veil.

- **Embracing narratives:** Numbers are crucial, but so are stories. They add depth to your understanding.

- **Constant evolution:** Strategies should be fluid. Challenge, iterate and adapt.

- **Sharing wisdom:** Talk about the veil of rationality. The more aware you are, the more holistic your collective decisions become.

There is so much richness that comes through stories and conversation. These things add to your wisdom and complement data and method. With practise, you will come to know when you are using rationality as a veil or truly deploying your wisdom to the problem.

CASE STUDY
UNLOCKING NEW
AVENUES FOR GROWTH

Let me share an example of something that has thankfully shifted beyond this veil. Back in the day there was a concept called 'social return on investment'. The idea was to quantify, often in dollars, the value of the social return of a service or social activity for every dollar invested into it. One dollar invested, eight dollars of social impact, and so forth. Projects developed massive spreadsheets to capture all the social impacts, and all the proxies used to measure social impact, in the pursuit of this magic—one in, eight out. One of my public speaking gigs was to be the dissenting voice against SROI, the prime reason being the rubbery nature of the proxies we would develop for measuring social impact—there was the appearance of science, but no real science.

After much debate the advisory industry has moved to impact assessment—a practice that blends hard data (not proxies) where it can be found, lived experience and the views of executives to try to deliver a qualitative and quantitative assessment of the impact any given initiative is having.

📖 Resources and references

Recent literary masterpieces, like Daniel Kahneman's *Thinking, Fast and Slow*, and the insights from behavioural economists like Richard Thaler, have pushed the envelope, challenging us to re-evaluate our notions of rationality. These are the frontier works pushing us to merge emotion with logic, making decisions that are not just smart, but profoundly insightful. For a deep dive, here are some great references:

Giridharadas, Anand. *Winners Take All: The Elite Charade of Changing the World*. New York: Alfred A. Knopf, 2018.

Harari, Yuval Noah. *Homo Deus: A Brief History of Tomorrow*. London: Harvill Secker, 2016.

Ito, Joi, and Jeff Howe. *Whiplash: How to Survive Our Faster Future*. New York: Grand Central Publishing, 2016.

Kahneman, Daniel. *Thinking, Fast and Slow*. New York: Farrar, Straus and Giroux, 2011.

Klein, Naomi. *On Fire: The (Burning) Case for a Green New Deal*. New York: Simon & Schuster, 2019.

O'Neil, Cathy. *Weapons of Math Destruction: How Big Data Increases Inequality and Threatens Democracy*. New York: Crown, 2016.

Raskino, Mark, and Graham Waller. *Digital to the Core: Remastering Leadership for Your Industry, Your Enterprise, and Yourself*. Stamford: Gartner, Inc., 2015.

Taleb, Nassim Nicholas. *Antifragile: Things That Gain from Disorder*. New York: Random House, 2012.

Thaler, Richard H., and Cass R. Sunstein. *Nudge: Improving Decisions About Health, Wealth, and Happiness.* New Haven: Yale University Press, 2008.

Zuboff, Shoshana. *The Age of Surveillance Capitalism: The Fight for a Human Future at the New Frontier of Power.* New York: PublicAffairs, 2019.

NAVIGATING CHANGE (CH)

STAKEHOLDER ENGAGEMENT (ST)

INNOVATION & ADAPTABILITY (IN)

FINANCIAL STABILITY (FS)

EMBRACING AMBIGUITY

TO EMBRACE ambiguity means to accept, tolerate or even appreciate situations, ideas or information that are unclear, uncertain or open to multiple interpretations. Are you comfortable in the absence of clear-cut answers or absolute certainty? Embracing ambiguity means you are willing to navigate through uncertainty, complexity and the unknown without feeling the need to resolve every uncertainty immediately. It's about being comfortable with being uncomfortable.

Pretend for a moment that you're the head of a space agency, and you've been tasked with planning a journey to find a habitable planet. You have limited resources, political pressures, and the unforgiving, unpredictable beast that is space itself to deal with. You have multiple candidate worlds to choose from, and some of the choices can't be made until you are already well into your journey. From engine failures to cosmic radiation, the list of things that could go wrong is extensive and largely unknown.

In a traditional strategic model, you'd plan for known risks and perhaps a few variables. But space laughs in the face of your plans. It's ambiguous, uncharted and dynamic. The real mastery in planning a mission—or any strategy in volatile conditions—is in designing for adaptability. You'll need a spacecraft that can adapt to unforeseen circumstances, a crew trained to handle unknown challenges, and a mission plan that allows for in-flight adjustments. The spacecraft must be a living entity that adapts, learns and evolves. How to do this? By embracing ambiguity.

In this mission, you must take off knowing that you cannot have the appropriate supplies to cover all eventualities. But you feel like you have the people and resources to make the right decisions and cope with the outcomes of those decisions—in the face of any challenge. This is what it means to embrace ambiguity.

Embracing ambiguity might sound like surrendering to chaos. But let's pause for a second and debunk that misconception. You see, ambiguity is often treated like a murky fog that must be cleared away for the path ahead to become visible. This is the traditional view, and it's deeply ingrained in our systems, our boardrooms and our decision-making processes. But here's the inconvenient truth: this attitude towards ambiguity might just be the most significant stumbling block we put in the way of innovative, responsive and agile strategic thinking.

Now, embracing ambiguity doesn't mean throwing all planning and rationality out the window. On the contrary, it complements these elements by adding a layer of fluidity. It encourages asking 'what if' questions. What if our assumptions are wrong? What if there's another way? It turns the spotlight towards adaptability and positions it as an asset, not a liability.

This approach reshapes not only how we strategise, but also how we execute and evaluate. It opens us up to the diversity of thought and breaks down the hierarchies that often stifle innovation. It's not about having all the answers, but about asking the right questions. It's about the journey of discovery where the act of finding out is as critical as the knowledge gained. As Rainer Maria Rilke perfectly encapsulated, 'Have patience with everything that remains unsolved in your heart. Live in the question.' So, as you ponder your next strategic move, dare to embrace the fog, the uncertainty, and the ambiguity. It just might be the clearest path forward.

⏱ When to use this Spark

So, when should you embrace ambiguity in strategic thinking? The answer is: more often than you'd think. When you're dealing with rapid technological changes, evolving customer needs or internal transformations like mergers and acquisitions, ambiguity is the name of the game. It provides a wellspring of untapped possibilities that can propel you into uncharted territories, which are often where the most significant opportunities lie. These aren't just words;

I've seen it unfold in real life and across sectors, from nonprofits wrestling with systemic change to governments grappling with policy impacts in a post-truth world.

And when is embracing ambiguity superior to other approaches? It outperforms when the game board is continually changing. In stable environments where cause and effect are linear and predictable, traditional planning might still hold sway. But let's be honest: how often do we find ourselves in such conditions these days? . . . Precisely.

How to use this Spark

To effectively blend psychological development with practical steps in embracing ambiguity for strategic thinking, incorporate the following steps:

1 **Self-reflection:** Begin by understanding your own and your team's psychological responses to ambiguity.

2 **Scenario flexibility:** Develop thinking around multiple scenarios, such as funding or policy changes, ensuring that each scenario has varying degrees of certainty (I call these 'crystal' through to 'fuzzy clear').

3 **Build the muscle:** Focus on enhancing cognitive flexibility and emotional intelligence (see the following tools).

4 **Pause:** The power of a pause! Learn to sit with ambiguity. Don't try to solve or conclude the process. Let it hang there for a while.

5 **Figure out how you will choose between options:** Develop the criteria or scorecard you will use to help you navigate towards a choice.

6 **Practise the nested 'if':** You may end up with ideas that are not just A or B, but rather 'if A, then C'. Embrace this as it is one of the pillars to strategic flexibility.

☑ The outcomes of using this Spark

What outcomes can you expect when you embrace ambiguity?

- **Increased resilience:** An ambiguous strategy is typically more flexible and adaptable, letting you pivot without much friction.

- **A culture of continuous learning and adaptation:** A strategy that embraces ambiguity accepts that the future is not a single point, but a range of possibilities. As J.K. Rowling put it, 'The consequences of our actions are always so complicated, so diverse, that predicting the future is a very difficult business indeed.'

- **New opportunities:** When we step forward into the unknown, previously unknown opportunities tend to present themselves.

- **Empowerment:** Leading people through ambiguous times can make them stronger. Coping with and surmounting such situations often requires many people doing complementary things, possibly in new ways. This breeds empowerment.

The courage of stepping into ambiguous situations is at the heart of human exploration and, while not without risk, is the pathway for greatest reward.

⚠ Dangers to beware of

I'd watch out for:

- **Overwhelm:** Some people don't cope with ambiguity... I won't point the finger at engineers, for example. Look out for stress indicators and if you see them, step in and show people how the process resolves.

- **Introspection:** Can I handle ambiguity or not, that is the question... Don't get stuck worrying about it; dive in and use the steps outlined earlier and you will soon find out.

- **Immobility:** Ambiguity doesn't mean you can't move forward. You are going to have to progress your strategic thinking, and this might mean making contingent decisions, rather than dithering.

- **Huddling:** Being the social creatures we are can lead teams to huddle together when faced with ambiguity and go round in circles about possibilities. It's crucial to keep the team focused on core strategic goals, preventing diversion into less relevant areas.

- **Psychological safety complacency:** Foster a psychologically safe environment that lets people be unsure and safe at the same time. Don't be complacent about the impact on your people as you step into the unknown.

By being mindful of these factors, you will be able to more effectively harness the potential of embracing ambiguity, ensuring that it leads to dynamic, resilient and psychologically informed strategic outcomes.

✂️ Muscle-building tips & techniques

If you want to hone your aptitude in the realm of embracing ambiguity through methods rather than gadgets, consider these progressive techniques:

- **Red teaming:** Think of this as an intellectual 'war game'. In red teaming, a separate group challenges the assumptions and plans of the main strategic team. It's an excellent method to consider multiple angles and address uncertainties head-on.

- **Double-loop learning:** Traditional single-loop learning asks, 'Are we doing things right?' Double-loop learning also asks, 'Are we doing the right things?' This self-reflective approach enables you to question underlying assumptions and paradigms, embracing ambiguity in your strategic objectives.

- **OODA Loop (Observe, Orient, Decide, Act):** Originally developed for military strategy, the OODA Loop is a cycle that emphasises rapid decision-making in ambiguous situations. The continuous loop facilitates agile strategy, allowing you to adapt to changing conditions swiftly.

- **Pre-mortem analysis:** Before fully implementing a strategy, conduct a hypothetical post-mortem to identify what could go wrong. This anticipatory method forces you to consider uncertainties and adapt your strategy to mitigate them.

- **Delphi Method:** Assemble a panel of experts and conduct multiple rounds of questioning on a strategic topic, refining the questions based on previous answers. This iterative method leverages collective intelligence to address ambiguous challenges.

- **Johari Window:** Employ the Johari Window to improve self-awareness and team dynamics. Developed by Joseph Luft and Harry Ingham, it's a simple but powerful tool for self-awareness and building trust. There are many resources online to show you how to use this tool.

Each of these methods requires a different mindset and skill set. Some will push you into the domain of uncomfortable unknowns, and others will invite you to engage in a degree of meta thinking about your strategies. But they all serve the same purpose: to arm you with the flexibility and foresight needed when charting paths through ambiguous terrains.

CASE STUDY
ADAPTIVE PLAN LEADS
TO REAL-LIFE BENEFITS

Imagine a nonprofit focused on environmental conservation. It had always operated on five-year strategic plans nailed to specific outcomes—until it embraced ambiguity. Its rigid planning model simply couldn't adapt to the fast-paced changes in climate patterns, governmental policies and technological advancements. Then it moved towards a fluid, adaptive model that allowed it to pivot more efficiently.

Within the first year, the organisation secured a high-profile partnership with a leading tech firm to deploy AI-powered wildlife tracking, something that was outside its original strategic purview. It became a hub for innovation and effectiveness, which had a ripple effect on its fundraising efforts. Its adaptability attracted not just funding, but the right kind of collaborative partnerships, transforming it from a local player to an influencer in global conservation circles. It knew the core of its mission, but was not fixated on the how; this allowed it to explore and seize opportunities as they emerged.

📖 Resources and references

Some deeper dive resources for you:

Carr, Nicholas. *The Shallows: What the Internet Is Doing to Our Brains.* New York: W.W. Norton & Company, 2010.

Case, Steve. *The Third Wave: An Entrepreneur's Vision of the Future.* New York: Simon & Schuster, 2016.

Harari, Yuval Noah. *Homo Deus: A Brief History of Tomorrow.* London: Harvill Secker, 2016.

Ito, Joi, and Jeff Howe. *Whiplash: How to Survive Our Faster Future.* New York: Grand Central Publishing, 2016.

Lanier, Jaron. *Ten Arguments for Deleting Your Social Media Accounts Right Now.* New York: Henry Holt and Co., 2018.

Newport, Cal. *Deep Work: Rules for Focused Success in a Distracted World.* New York: Grand Central Publishing, 2016.

Ries, Eric. *The Startup Way: How Modern Companies Use Entrepreneurial Management to Transform Culture and Drive Long-Term Growth.* New York: Currency, 2017.

Scott, Galloway. *The Four: The Hidden DNA of Amazon, Apple, Facebook, and Google.* New York: Penguin Press, 2017.

Taleb, Nassim Nicholas. *Skin in the Game: Hidden Asymmetries in Daily Life.* New York: Random House, 2018.

Zimbardo, Philip, and John Boyd. *The Time Paradox: The New Psychology of Time That Will Change Your Life*. New York: Free Press, 2008.

RESOURCE MANAGEMENT (RE)

FINANCIAL STABILITY (FS)

SYSTEM REFORM (SR)

RISK MANAGEMENT (RI)

CRITICAL THINKING

'CRITICAL THINKING' is a term that's bandied about so frequently in boardrooms, classrooms and intellectual circles that one might think it's just another buzzword. Do people mean 'Get your emotions out of the way' or do they mean 'Be objective' or do they mean 'I don't like what you are saying!'?

So, what is critical thinking? At its core, it's the ability to think clearly and rationally, understanding the logical connection between ideas. It's about being active (not reactive) in your learning processes, and it involves being open-minded, inquisitive and able to think in a reasoned way.

Imagine an interstellar mission launched by Earth to explore a distant exoplanet in the Alpha Centauri system, believed to harbour life. As thrilling as this venture might be, embarking on such a journey based on mere assumptions could be catastrophic.

Instead, the mission team, having worked with some of the best strategic minds, engages in critical thinking. They question every piece of data: Is the planet's atmosphere truly hospitable? Are the signals we detected indicative of life or just cosmic noise? What are the risks of long-duration space travel, and how do we mitigate them?

By critically analysing each factor, the team unveils nuances. They find that the exoplanet, while having an atmosphere, has extreme weather patterns. The signals, upon deeper analysis, show patterns different from biological life, suggesting natural cosmic phenomena. Recognising these ambiguities, the mission pivots from a colonisation focus to a scientific reconnaissance one.

In the vastness of space, where mistakes can be irreversible, critical thinking becomes the beacon and guides humanity in its quest to explore the cosmos, ensuring that our interstellar ambitions are grounded in reason, evidence and a thirst for truth.

Critical thinking is not merely accumulating information. It's about understanding, analysis, synthesis and evaluation. It's the process of actively and skilfully conceptualising, applying, analysing, synthesising and evaluating information to reach a conclusion.

In the realm of strategic thinking, especially for organisations and Boards I've had the privilege to collaborate with, critical thinking serves as the backbone of any strategic plan. It's the difference between a strategy that's merely good and one that's truly transformative.

🕐 When to use this Spark

Compared to other concepts, critical thinking stands out in situations where there's a high degree of complexity or ambiguity. While tools like directional thinking provide a clear path, critical thinking ensures that the path chosen stands up to scrutiny. It's the process that questions, refines and perfects the direction.

From the initial stages of understanding the problem, throughout the ideation process, and right up to the evaluation of outcomes, critical thinking ensures that decisions are grounded in reason, evidence and a deep understanding of the nuances of the situation.

📋 How to use this Spark

To embed critical thinking into your strategic thinking capability, follow these steps:

1 **Foster a questioning mindset:** Encourage yourself and your team to consistently question assumptions and existing beliefs. This starts with cultivating a culture where enquiry is valued.

2 **Gather diverse information:** Actively seek varied sources of information to ensure a well-rounded understanding of the issues at hand. This involves looking beyond familiar channels to gather diverse perspectives.

3   **Analyse information objectively:** Critically evaluate the information gathered. This includes assessing the credibility of sources, analysing data for biases and understanding the limitations of your knowledge.

4   **Encourage debate and discussion:** Create forums for open discussion where different viewpoints can be debated. This helps in challenging perspectives and uncovering hidden assumptions.

5   **Develop logical reasoning skills:** Regularly practise and apply logical reasoning in your decision-making process, ensuring conclusions are well founded.

6   **Reflect and refine:** Post-decision, reflect on the thinking process and outcomes. Identify areas for improvement in your critical thinking approach.

7   **Continuous learning and development:** Commit to ongoing learning and development in critical thinking skills, keeping abreast of new methods and approaches.

By systematically integrating these steps into your strategic planning process, you ensure decisions are not just intuitive but also backed by rigorous, critical thinking, essential for robust and effective strategies.

☑ The outcomes of using this Spark

The benefits of integrating critical thinking into strategy are manifold. It allows organisations to navigate complex problems, see beyond superficial challenges, and devise solutions that are both innovative and effective. Let's look at some of those benefits:

- **Creativity:** Contrary to popular belief, critical thinking and creativity are not mutually exclusive. Critical thinking can spark innovation. By debating in an exploratory way, we open up our minds to new ideas that can make a real difference to our social problems.

- **Effective solutions:** Critical thinking enables a more structured approach to problem-solving. By systematically breaking down complex issues we can identify nub or root causes and interactions, which in turn leads us to more efficient and sometimes more targeted solutions. This is particularly crucial in the for-purpose sector, where resources are limited and impact maximisation is the goal.

- **Resilient strategies:** The flow of critical thinking involves stress testing and debate. This testing leads to better decisions and instils confidence in those decisions. This confidence helps bind people as they go into the unknown.

- **Enhanced communication:** A natural outcome of stress testing is clarity and precision in communication. With clarity, nonprofits can avoid misunderstandings and inefficiencies, which is crucial when working with complex social issues and when rallying support is essential.

In short, this Spark is about crystallising and clarifying your thinking through the crucible of structure, debate and stress testing. Don't take rebuttal as rejection—rather, take it as a sign you are on the right path in the first place!

⚠ Dangers to beware of

When employing critical thinking to develop strategy, it's important to be mindful of certain pitfalls:

- **Over-analysis:** Excessive analysis can lead to decision paralysis, where overthinking impedes timely action.

- **Confirmation bias:** There's a risk of favouring information that confirms pre-existing beliefs or hypotheses. It's crucial to objectively evaluate all available information.

- **Lack of diverse perspectives:** Critical thinking requires consideration of multiple viewpoints. Neglecting diverse perspectives can result in a narrow understanding of the issue at hand.

- **Misinterpreting information:** There's always a danger of misinterpreting data or information, especially in complex or ambiguous situations.

- **Emotional overlook:** While critical thinking focuses on rationality, it's important not to completely dismiss emotional intelligence, which can provide valuable insights.

- **Communication breakdown:** Robust critical thinking can be misperceived as criticism by others. Effective communication is key to ensuring that critical analysis is constructive and collaborative.

- **Overconfidence:** Successful critical thinking can lead to overconfidence, making it important to remain open to new information and perspectives.

By being aware of these challenges, critical thinking can be more effectively integrated into strategic planning, ensuring it enhances rather than hinders decision-making.

🛠 Capability-building tools & techniques

For those intrigued by the profound influence of critical thinking on strategy, there are several psychological tools that can be harnessed to sharpen this skill:

- **Socratic questioning:** This involves asking open-ended questions that challenge assumptions and promote deeper understanding.

- **The five whys:** A technique that involves asking 'Why?' five times in succession to uncover the root cause of a problem.

- **Pre-mortems:** Before launching any project or strategy, engage in a cognitive exercise to predict what could go wrong, and plan accordingly.

- **Decision frameworks:** Utilise models like SWOT, PESTLE, or even custom frameworks to dissect challenges from multiple angles.

- **Reflect and adapt:** Post-implementation, set aside time to examine what worked, what didn't and why, to inform future strategies.

As the renowned philosopher Confucius noted, 'Real knowledge is to know the extent of one's ignorance.' This encapsulates the spirit of critical thinking. To think critically is to acknowledge what we don't know and to be driven by a relentless pursuit of truth, clarity and understanding.

CASE STUDY
A NONPROFIT'S AWAKENING
WITH CRITICAL THINKING

In the heart of Adelaide, YouthAlive, a nonprofit passionate about youth development, was facing dwindling engagement rates. Traditional outreach methods were failing, and its programs were losing traction. Driven by their commitment to the cause, the leadership sought to reinvent their approach.

Incorporating a critical thinking framework, they began questioning every facet of their operation. Why were certain programs underperforming? Were their assumptions about the youth community outdated? What evidence did they have to support their current strategies? Their team, many of whom I had the honour to work with, began to deconstruct, analyse and critically assess their methodologies.

The revelations were transformative. They found that their initiatives, though well-intentioned, were not resonating with the evolving interests and challenges of the youth. Their programs were based on dated assumptions rather than current realities.

Leveraging this newfound clarity, YouthAlive overhauled its programs. It initiated evidence-based interventions, co-designed projects with the youth, and forged partnerships with local schools and digital platforms to enhance outreach.

The results were astounding. Within two years, Youth-Alive saw a seventy per cent surge in youth engagement and carved a niche for itself as an innovator in youth development in Adelaide. Its embrace of critical thinking transformed a looming crisis into a remarkable success story.

Resources and references

For further exploration:

Brookfield, Stephen D. *Developing Critical Thinkers.* Jossey-Bass, 1987.

Dewey, John. *How We Think.* D.C. Heath, 1910.

Facione, Peter A. *Critical Thinking: What It Is and Why It Counts.* Measured Reasons and the California Academic Press, 2010.

Kahneman, Daniel. *Thinking, Fast and Slow.* Farrar, Straus and Giroux, 2011.

Moon, Jennifer. *Critical Thinking: An Exploration of Theory and Practice.* Routledge, 2008.

Paul, Richard, and Linda Elder. *The Miniature Guide to Critical Thinking.* Foundation for Critical Thinking, 2006.

Ruggiero, Vincent Ryan. *The Art of Thinking: A Guide to Critical and Creative Thought.* Pearson, 2011.

Sagan, Carl. *The Demon-Haunted World: Science as a Candle in the Dark.* Random House, 1995.

Senge, Peter. *The Fifth Discipline.* Doubleday, 1990.

Toulmin, Stephen. *The Uses of Argument.* Cambridge University Press, 1958.

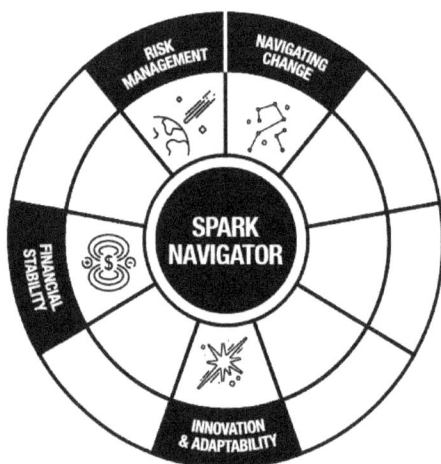

NAVIGATING CHANGE (CH)

INNOVATION & ADAPTABILITY (IN)

FINANCIAL STABILITY (FS)

RISK MANAGEMENT (RI)

CONSTRUCTIVE
SCEPTICISM

SCEPTICAL THINKING is a component of critical thinking that emphasises questioning and doubting claims until substantial evidence is provided. It's a nuanced form of critical thinking, and it's this nuance that is important in strategic thinking.

Consider for a moment that we're on the brink of establishing humanity's first colony on Mars. Most space agencies have the enthusiasm they need and the technology mapped out, but outer space is unpredictable and uncharted. How can the brains and power behind these tentative attempts to inhabit another planet be sure they have thought of everything?

Now visualise an interstellar council, strategising about Mars's terraformation. On face value, the process seems straightforward—introduce oxygen, cultivate flora and stabilise temperatures. But is it? What questions have not been asked? The forward-thinking interstellar council decides to use constructive scepticism to check their strategy. They might ask: 'What if Mars has dormant microbial life? What's the ethical stance on potentially wiping out an alien microecosystem?'

The council is not trying to hinder progress, but ensure that every strategic move in space, where the unknown is the norm, is made after rigorous questioning. This form of critical inquiry might be the difference between a thriving Martian colony and one that inadvertently triggers interstellar ecological catastrophes. In the vastness of space, where each decision carries cosmic weight, embracing a sceptical lens is not just wise; it's a necessity for the survival and ethical evolution of humankind among the stars.

Contrary to popular belief, scepticism isn't about dismissing ideas or opportunities out of hand; it's about asking incisive questions, examining data and evaluating the implications. Scepticism is to thought what antibodies are to the immune system—a defence mechanism against toxic or ill-considered ideas.

Rather than taking information at face value, it nudges us to dig deeper, to challenge, and to understand the nuances. As Richard Feynman aptly put it, 'I would rather have questions that can't be answered than answers that can't be questioned.'

But before we dive on in, a cautionary note. One I seem to tell all my new consultants. It's easy to say, 'Yeah, yeah, I know about this,' and skip past. The power of this Spark is that it forces you to stop and insert a question into your busy day and busy thinking at a point where you might just accept what's in front of you. This is a new cognitive step that needs practise and nurturing ... without becoming a pain to everyone around you!

🕐 When to use this Spark

When do we employ this vital tool in our strategic thinking arsenal? In boardrooms, when stakeholders present data, it's our duty to approach it with a balanced mix of acceptance and scrutiny. When new partnerships or collaborations are on the horizon, constructive scepticism ensures we're not just seeing the opportunity, but also the potential challenges. It's a protective mechanism that prevents tunnel vision and the allure of attractive yet hollow propositions.

📝 How to use this Spark

This approach forces us to ask questions. This asking is especially prudent in the resource-constrained for-purpose sector. It forces us to squeeze every thinking drop out of ourselves in our strategic thinking, which in turn leads to more effective, sustainable and mission-aligned outcomes, crucial for nonprofit success.

Here is the mental approach I use when wanting to deploy this Spark. It is based on the sceptic method and rooted in philosophical scepticism:

1   **Identify and question key assertions:** Begin by breaking down what is in front of you and looking for pivotal assertions or facts. Question the validity of these assertions. Especially organisational sacred cows.

2   **Get to the evidence:** Once you have picked your target 'fact', seek out the evidence. Analyse the evidence supporting these facts. Scrutinise the quality, source and relevance of the evidence presented. I can't tell you how many times I find that the 'fact' is really a long-gone team member's opinion.

3   **Identify assumptions:** Uncover and challenge the assumptions supporting these facts. This helps in understanding the foundational beliefs that need re-examination.

4   **Suspend judgement:** Maintain a stance of suspension of judgement in the absence of conclusive evidence. Avoid jumping to conclusions based on insufficient information.

5   **Develop your view:** Confirm the fact or re-organise the evidence and assumptions into a new 'fact' or insight.

6   **Evaluate logical consistency:** Assess the logical coherence of the new or validated insight. Identify any fallacies or inconsistencies in reasoning.

7   **Practise intellectual humility:** Recognise the limits of your knowledge and remain open to new information and correction.

Constructive scepticism is a powerful tool in strategic thinking, encouraging a thorough and critical evaluation of information, leading to more informed and rational decision-making.

☑ The outcomes of using this Spark

There are direct benefits from using this Spark in your strategic thinking. Here are some relevant to the strategic pillars of a for-purpose workplace:

- **Greater social impact:** Deep questioning uncovers the most effective ways to allocate resources, ensuring that impact strategies are focused and efficient, directly addressing the needs of beneficiaries.

- **Deeper donor engagement:** A sceptical approach to understanding donor behaviours and preferences leads to more effective donor engagement strategies, ensuring alignment with donor expectations and increased funding.

- **Accurate evaluation:** Regularly questioning and evaluating program effectiveness helps in refining and adapting nonprofit initiatives, ensuring they achieve their intended impact.

- **Strategic advocacy:** Challenging assumptions around advocacy efforts can reveal innovative approaches to policy change and community engagement, enhancing the nonprofit's influence and reach.

- **Better volunteer management:** Applying scepticism to volunteer engagement and management strategies ensures that volunteers are effectively utilised, their preferences are understood and their contributions align with organisational goals.

In the nonprofit sector, constructive scepticism in strategic planning ensures not only that resources are used effectively, but also that the organisation remains agile, impactful and aligned with its mission and stakeholder needs.

⚠️ Dangers to beware of

When employing constructive scepticism in strategic thinking, caution is required. Aside from becoming a total dick, disliked by everyone, watch out for these things:

- **Cynicism:** While scepticism is healthy, it's important not to slide into cynicism. Scepticism questions and seeks evidence; cynicism outright dismisses and distrusts.

- **Decision paralysis:** Excessive questioning can lead to analysis paralysis, where progress is endlessly deferred. It's crucial to find the balance between healthy scepticism and progress in your thinking.

- **Dismissing established knowledge:** While it's important to question, we should also respect and consider the value of established knowledge and expertise.

- **Non-constructive dialogue:** Scepticism should be exercised in a way that fosters open and constructive dialogue, not conflict or dismissiveness.

- **Overlooking consensus:** Sometimes, consensus is necessary. Over-scepticism can disrupt the process of reaching a common understanding or agreement.

- **Isolation:** Excessive scepticism might isolate you from others, especially if it's perceived as unyielding or confrontational.

By being aware of these potential pitfalls, you will ensure that using constructive scepticism in strategic thinking remains balanced, productive, and aligned with broader collaborative and decision-making processes.

Capability-building tools & techniques

For those looking to amplify their skill set in this domain, here are six tools that, when embraced, can foster a more profound grasp of this concept:

- **Red team strategy exercises:** Adopted from military war games, this involves creating a team whose sole purpose is to challenge an organisation's strategy or plan. By actively seeking to find holes or vulnerabilities, it forces the primary team to think critically and defend its choices, promoting a sceptical mindset.

- **Futures thinking workshops:** Engage in workshops that delve into speculative futures. By contemplating multiple potential scenarios for the future, one learns to question the present. Organisations like the School of International Futures offer such workshops.

- **'Kill the company' brainstorming sessions:** Popularised by innovation expert Lisa Bodell, this exercise involves teams brainstorming ways in which they would put their own company out of business. This reverse psychology approach helps identify blind spots in current strategies and cultivates a questioning approach.

- **Deep dive immersions:** Sometimes, stepping out of your environment can foster scepticism. Embark on immersion trips into entirely different industries or cultures. The exposure to different ways of thinking and doing can spark a questioning mindset when you return to your domain.

- **Digital detox retreats:** In our information-saturated age, taking time to disconnect can sharpen critical thinking. Retreats that emphasise reflection, devoid of technology, can allow you to sift through information more sceptically when you reconnect.

- **Devil's advocate debates:** Regularly organise debates where participants are randomly assigned positions, even if they don't personally believe in them. Defending or arguing against a particular stance hones the skill of looking at issues from multiple perspectives and encourages questioning of commonly held beliefs.

Embracing these unconventional methods and tools, challenging though they may be, can undoubtedly amplify your constructive scepticism skills. They compel us to step out of our comfort zones, question our beliefs, and foster an environment where strategic thinking thrives on a mix of trust and enquiry.

CASE STUDY
TRIUMPH THROUGH
CONSTRUCTIVE SCEPTICISM

In Melbourne's heart, a nonprofit dedicated to providing education for underprivileged children faced a strategic crossroads. Yearly donations were in decline, and the traditional methods of fundraising were yielding diminishing returns. Enter the application of constructive scepticism.

Instead of following the usual route of revising its marketing strategies, it decided to critically question every operational facet. It engaged in red team strategy exercises, where a separate team played the role of critics to the organisation's fundraising approaches. The results were enlightening. The red team pinpointed not just superficial issues, but deep-rooted strategic flaws that had been overlooked.

This self-imposed sceptical scrutiny led to the discovery that their core audience—previous donors—felt disconnected from the organisation's mission. Responding to this insight, the nonprofit initiated 'deep dive immersions', inviting donors to spend a day understanding the nonprofit's work, bridging the empathy gap.

The results? Within a year, not only did donations see an uptick, but there was a stronger sense of community and connection between the donors and the nonprofit. By harnessing the power of constructive scepticism, the organisation was not just able to sustain, but to thrive and amplify its impact.

📖 Resources and references

Here are some resources for you to deep dive into this world:

Facione, Peter A. *Critical Thinking: What It Is and Why It Counts.* Measured Reasons and the California Academic Press, 2011.

Gilbert, Daniel T. *Stumbling on Happiness.* Knopf, New York, NY, 2006.

Jha, Alok. *The Irrational Ape: Why Flawed Logic Puts Us All at Risk and How Critical Thinking Can Save the World.* Simon & Schuster UK, 2019.

Kahneman, Daniel. *Thinking, Fast and Slow.* Farrar, Straus and Giroux, New York, NY, 2011.

Oakley, Barbara A. *Mindshift: Break Through Obstacles to Learning and Discover Your Hidden Potential.* TarcherPerigee, 2017.

Paul, Richard, and Linda Elder. *The Miniature Guide to Critical Thinking: Concepts & Tools.* Foundation for Critical Thinking, 2009.

Popper, Karl. *The Logic of Scientific Discovery.* Routledge Classics, London, 2002.

Sagan, Carl. *The Demon-Haunted World: Science as a Candle in the Dark.* Random House, New York, NY, 1996.

Shermer, Michael. *The Believing Brain: From Ghosts and Gods to Politics and Conspiracies—How We Construct Beliefs and Reinforce Them as Truths.* Times Books, 2011.

Taleb, Nassim Nicholas. *The Black Swan: The Impact of the Highly Improbable.* New York: Random House, 2007.

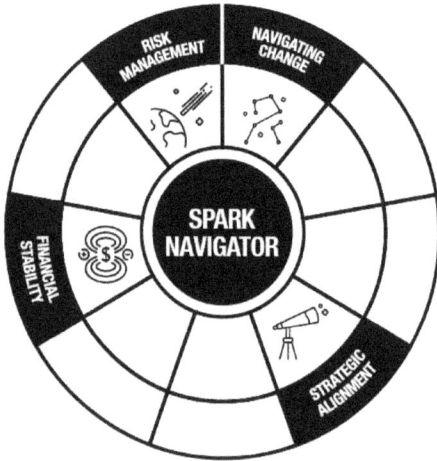

NAVIGATING CHANGE (CH)
STRATEGIC ALIGNMENT (AL)
FINANCIAL STABILITY (FS)
RISK MANAGEMENT (RI)

BALANCING LONG AND SHORT TERM

IN THE ceaseless ebb and flow of organisational priorities, the strength and resilience of a strategy often hinge on its ability to dance gracefully between the now and the next. As leaders, as thinkers, as dreamers, our task is to ensure that while we build bridges to a luminous future, we don't lose sight of the land we stand upon.

Imagine a civilisation on a distant exoplanet named Nebula-9. Nebula-9 faces an intriguing challenge. Its planet is in the path of an oncoming asteroid shower, expected to hit in about 100 years. But it's also grappling with immediate energy shortages affecting daily life.

The only option is to initiate a dual strategy. For the immediate challenge, it channels resources to tap into the energy of its blue star using cutting-edge technology, ensuring it doesn't plummet into an energy crisis. Simultaneously, understanding the gravity of the impending asteroid shower, it begins constructing robust underground cities and researching asteroid deflection techniques.

It's a dance of strategy, as immediate needs harmonise with future planning. This ensures that while today's Nebulan thrives, the future Nebulan has a safe planet to call home. It's a cosmic reminder: whether you're on Earth or a planet light years away, the balance between addressing the now and preparing for the future remains a universal, strategic constant.

The concept of balancing long and short term in strategic thinking is, broadly, pretty obvious. But there is a nuance to this Spark that I want to share with you. That is, that this balance is not a question of priorities (short-term imperatives versus long-term goals). The nuance is more a generational thought.

'A society grows great when old (people) plant trees whose shade they know they shall never sit in.' This ancient Greek proverb encapsulates the idea of selflessness and investing in the future, emphasising the importance of doing work that benefits future generations, even if one does not personally reap the rewards. The proverb highlights the virtue of thinking long term and contributing to the greater good without expecting immediate personal gain.

Understand that your strategic thinking will need to hit short-term goals, but also undertake projects and activities now whose payback may happen well beyond your tenure.

In the profound words of Peter Drucker, 'The best way to predict the future is to create it.'

(clock icon) When to use this Spark

For a nonprofit, the role of balancing short- and long-term thinking in strategic thinking is vital in several key areas. These include devising fundraising strategies, developing programs to address community needs, formulating partnership strategies and responding to a crisis, integrating volunteer strategies and undertaking strategic planning for advocacy and policy.

In these areas, strategic thinking in a nonprofit context must adeptly navigate the immediate challenges while maintaining a clear focus on the long-term mission, ensuring decisions made today support the organisation's future sustainability and impact.

(notepad icon) How to use this Spark

To balance short- and long-term thinking in my strategic approach, I take the following specific steps (much of this is the work you would do in developing an outcomes framework, adapted to your strategic thinking):

1 **Clearly define long-term objectives and impact:** The former is about what you will create, the latter is about the meta social impact you will contribute to. For example, ending avoidable blindness will deliver social and economic benefit.

2 **Work backwards:** Plot a pathway from long to short that does two things. First, it develops the runway of initiatives to deliver the long-term outcome. Second, it drops into the thinking specific actions needed in each period, based on what we expect to happen in that period.

3 **Sense check:** Do you have the resources, capability and capacity to deliver this dual track?

4 **Maintain transparent communication:** Keep all stakeholders informed about the dual-focus approach, clarifying how short-term achievements lay the groundwork for long-term success.

5 **Be adaptable in tactics:** Stay flexible, ready to recalibrate short-term actions to stay aligned with your long-term vision.

6 **Foster dual-focused culture:** Encourage a team mindset that values immediate results while keeping an eye on future opportunities and challenges.

Following these steps ensures a holistic strategic approach, which effectively manages immediate needs while steadily working towards long-term aspirations.

☑ The outcomes of using this Spark

By balancing short- and long-term thinking in your strategic planning, you can expect several key outcomes:

- **Optimised resource use:** Looking in both horizons will help you understand what resources you will have over time and allocate them more effectively, ensuring immediate needs are met without compromising long-term initiatives.

- **Greater flexibility:** By contrast, thinking short term while knowing what the long-term view is will help you draw forward (or defer) resources to deal with immediate challenges while keeping your long-term vision on track.

- **Enhanced stakeholder engagement:** Doing what you say you will over time is one of the best ways to build trust. Balancing these perspectives will satisfy immediate stakeholder needs while steadily working towards future benefits, leading to increased trust and support.

- **Resilient strategic framework:** Long-run resilience comes from more than just resource management. The whole system of decision-making and execution needs to be able to withstand short-term shocks and prepare for longer-term trends. This dual view greatly assists here.

- **Informed and comprehensive decision-making:** Decisions will be grounded in a clearer understanding of their immediate and future impacts.

- **Consistent alignment with mission:** Regularly aligning short-term tactics with your long-term mission ensures cohesive progress towards your overarching goals.

Implementing this dual approach ensures you are not just responsive to current demands, but also proactively shaping a robust and sustainable future.

⚠ Dangers to beware of

When employing the balance of short- and long-term thinking in strategic planning, watch out for:

- **Neglected immediate needs:** Overemphasis on long-term goals shouldn't overshadow urgent short-term necessities.

- **Overlooked long-term vision:** Conversely, being too caught up in immediate tasks can derail you from your long-term objectives.

- **Resource misallocation:** Ensure resources are effectively distributed to support both current operations and future initiatives.

- **Analysis paralysis:** Striving for perfect balance can lead to indecision. Stay decisive even when navigating this duality.

- **Stakeholder misalignment:** Keep stakeholders aligned and informed about the rationale behind balancing short- and long-term priorities.

The tip here is to take a balanced view when it comes to time. Don't be too focused on either long or short term; often, action is better than standing on the curb.

🛠 Capability-building tools & techniques

How can one cultivate this dexterity in strategic thinking? Try these methods:

- **Immersive role-playing games (RPGs):** This might appear left-of-field, but consider the mechanics of a complex RPG like *Dungeons & Dragons*. Players must make decisions that serve their immediate needs while also plotting a course for future success. Participating in such games sharpens one's ability to weigh the immediate against the future, making choices in the present that set up for long-term strategy.

- **Future backwards technique:** This method, initially from the Cynefin framework, encourages participants to imagine a worst-case future scenario and then work backwards to the present, identifying decisions and pivot points that led to that outcome. By then reversing the process to envision the path to an ideal future, you cultivate a dual perspective on short- and long-term effects.

- **Time-capsule exercise:** Create a time capsule for your organisation or personal goals. What would you want to tell your future self or future stakeholders? This exercise forces a tangible confrontation with the future, compelling you to consider what short-term actions will have long-standing ramifications.

- **10/10/10 rule exploration:** Introduced by Suzy Welch, this rule asks you to consider the consequences of a decision ten minutes, ten months and ten years from now. By forcing yourself into these different temporal headspaces, you can more effectively weigh the immediate versus the distant implications of a choice.

- **Engaging with futurists' media:** Consume podcasts, blogs or seminars from futurists like Amy Webb or Jane McGonigal. These experts grapple with forecasting and its implications, and their speculative methods can offer fresh techniques for balancing immediate needs with future contingencies.

- **Scarcity simulations:** Engage in exercises or simulations where resources (like time or money) are intentionally limited. This scarcity forces prioritisation, making it necessary to choose actions that serve both immediate survival and future growth.

By employing these tools, one not only grasps the theory behind balancing the immediate and the eventual, but also develops an instinctive feel for it.

After all, in the rapidly evolving landscapes of today's challenges, sometimes it's that instinct, that gut feel honed by diverse experiences, that guides us most effectively.

CASE STUDY
THE LIFELONG
LEARNING INITIATIVE

In the heart of Melbourne, the nonprofit Lifelong Learning Initiative (LLI) was confronting a paradox. Founded on the principle that education can change lives, LLI had always prioritised immediate projects: a literacy program here, a series of workshops there. However, it was haunted by a lingering question: while it was making an impact now, was it truly setting the stage for long-term, transformative change?

Adopting the strategy of balancing long and short term, LLI began by engaging in the time-capsule exercise. It envisaged what it would like the community's educational landscape to look like in a decade, penning letters to future stakeholders. This future-focused reflection highlighted gaps in its strategy. While it was addressing the educational needs of the moment, it wasn't necessarily laying the groundwork for a continually evolving, self-sustaining educational ecosystem.

LLI then shifted gears. It continued its short-term programs but paired them with long-term investments, like mentorship programs where today's learners could become tomorrow's teachers, and partnerships with local businesses to ensure evolving curricula aligned with real-world needs.

Today, LLI's efforts are reaping fruits. Immediate educational needs are being met, but there's also an eco-system ensuring that the educational aspirations of the community evolve and are addressed in perpetuity.

📖 Resources and references

For the voraciously curious minds, here are ten edgy, non-mainstream resources that can offer fresh perspectives on the art of balancing the immediate with the eventual:

Carse, James P. *Finite and Infinite Games.* New York: Free Press, 1986.

Christensen, Clayton M. *The Innovator's Dilemma: When New Technologies Cause Great Firms to Fail.* Boston: Harvard Business Review Press, 1997.

Colonna, Jerry. *Reboot: Leadership and the Art of Growing Up.* New York: HarperBusiness, 2019.

Duke, Annie. *Thinking in Bets: Making Smarter Decisions When You Don't Have All the Facts.* New York: Portfolio, 2018.

Ghemawat, Pankaj. *Long Views: The 3+2 Approach to Mastering Global Business.* New York: McGraw-Hill, 2010.

Klein, Gary. *Seeing What Others Don't: The Remarkable Ways We Gain Insights.* New York: PublicAffairs, 2013.

Ries, Eric. *The Lean Startup: How Today's Entrepreneurs Use Continuous Innovation to Create Radically Successful Businesses.* New York: Crown Business, 2011.

Taleb, Nassim Nicholas. *Antifragile: Things That Gain from Disorder.* New York: Random House, 2012.

Tetlock, Philip E., and Dan M. Gardner. *Superforecasting: The Art and Science of Prediction.* New York: Crown Publishing, 2015.

van der Heijden, Kees. *Scenarios: The Art of Strategic Conversation.* Chichester: Wiley, 1996.

STAKEHOLDER ENGAGEMENT (ST)

STRATEGIC ALIGNMENT (AL)

CULTURE & LEADERSHIP (CL)

STRATEGIC AUTHENTICITY

STRATEGIC AUTHENTICITY is the deliberate and purposeful alignment of an organisation's strategic decisions, actions and communications with its core values, mission and identity. It ensures that the organisation's outward-facing image, as well as internal operations, reflect an honest and genuine commitment to its stated principles.

Let's take a leap from Earth and visit outer space. Imagine we're strategising for a space exploration mission. It's not about racing to be the first to discover a new exoplanet or mining the most resources from an asteroid. No, the mission is fuelled by the genuine pursuit of knowledge, a deep-rooted curiosity about the universe, and the ambition to push the boundaries of human capability.

The strategy might include developing new technologies for sustainable life-support systems, but it's authentically committed to the broader, nobler cause of advancing human understanding of space. We're not just exploring for the sake of economic or political gains; we're doing it to answer the existential questions that have haunted humanity since we first looked up at the night sky.

In this space odyssey, every team member, from the engineers to the astronauts, is aligned with the mission's authentic objective. Decisions, whether about allocating resources or executing complex manoeuvres, emanate from this core purpose. As a result, the mission doesn't just make history; it elevates humanity's quest for understanding our place in the universe. That's strategic authenticity, not just in a boardroom on Earth, but across the cosmic expanse.

In essence, strategic authenticity is about being 'aligned' from the inside out. It's the deliberate alignment of an organisation's history, beliefs and purpose with its strategies and actions. Now, isn't that what all good leaders would be doing anyway?

This is about doing the right things, guided by an unwavering commitment to genuine intent and ethical congruence. In the words of Shakespeare, 'This above all: to thine own self be true.'

This authenticity not only guides internal decisions, but also acts as a beacon that attracts stakeholders and communities aligned with the same purpose.

🕐 When to use this Spark

When should organisations invoke strategic authenticity in their decision-making? When they're at a crossroads, when immediate gains seem to overshadow long-term values, and especially when strategies seem to deviate from core beliefs. The outcome is multifaceted: genuine stakeholder relationships, ethical satisfaction and often, paradoxically, even economic benefits.

How does strategic authenticity compare to other strategic paradigms? While many strategic frameworks offer tools and techniques, strategic authenticity is foundational. It's the moral compass guiding the use of these tools, ensuring actions resonate deeply, both internally and externally. As the insightful resource *Dare to Lead* by Brené Brown emphasises, leadership isn't about having the right answers but about having the right questions, rooted in authenticity.

📋 How to use this Spark

To develop strategic authenticity in strategic thinking, follow these steps:

1 **Shine your light:** Clearly identify and map the belief, purpose and problem you have been solving. Figure out what has been working and why.

2   **Shine this light on your thinking:** The way to do this is to ask, 'Is there anything about our strategic thoughts that runs counter to this authenticity? Is there anything we would need to do or become that is not aligned with this?'

3   **Practise transparent communication:** Maintain openness in all communications, reinforcing the authenticity of your strategic intentions. This is even more important when the strategic thinking requires a shift away from a successful past.

4   **Regularly revisit and reflect:** Consistently revisit your strategies to ensure they stay true to your core.

5   **Foster a values-driven culture:** Encourage a culture within the organisation that prioritises values in decision-making.

6   **Evaluate impact:** Regularly assess the impact of your strategies against your purpose, adjusting as needed to maintain alignment and authenticity.

By systematically incorporating these steps, strategic thinking becomes deeply rooted in authenticity, resonating with both internal and external stakeholders.

☑ The outcomes of using this Spark

Integrating strategic authenticity into a nonprofit's strategic thinking leads to several practical outcomes:

- **Enhanced community trust:** By aligning strategies with core values, you build deeper trust with donors, demonstrating commitment to your purpose.

- **Increased stakeholder engagement:** Authenticity in your strategic approach gives stakeholders confidence that over the long run, you will build stronger connection to your purpose and make clear their role, enhancing engagement and support.

- **Sustainable funding:** Staying true to your purpose can attract and retain funders who are aligned with your values, leading to more sustainable financial support.

- **Consistent organisational identity:** This approach reinforces a clear and consistent identity, helping to differentiate your nonprofit in a crowded sector.

- **Improved program effectiveness:** Strategies that are authentically aligned with your purpose are more likely to effectively address community needs, leading to greater impact.

- **Staff and volunteer satisfaction:** An authentic strategic idea increases satisfaction and morale among staff and volunteers, as they feel part of a purpose-driven organisation they know.

By focusing on strategic authenticity, your nonprofit not only stays true to its mission but also builds a stronger, more impactful and sustainable organisation.

⚠️ Dangers to beware of

In embedding strategic authenticity into strategic thinking, especially within a nonprofit context, several key factors require vigilance:

- **Misalignment with stakeholder expectations:** While staying true to your purpose, ensure strategies also align with expectations and funding trends, balancing authenticity with practical funding needs.

- **Purpose drift:** Be vigilant against straying from your core purpose in pursuit of funding or partnerships, which can lead to a loss of identity and supporter trust.

- **Overemphasis on branding:** While authenticity enhances branding, avoid focusing so heavily on image and the 'you' of the past that it overshadows substance and current action towards impact.

- **Stakeholder misinterpretation:** Ensure transparent communications are clear and accurately reflect your intentions, avoiding misinterpretations that could harm your reputation in times of change.

- **Conflict between values and practicality:** When organisational values clash with practical or operational necessities, seek creative solutions that uphold your ethos without compromising effectiveness.

- **Jumping on the bandwagon:** Be cautious about jumping onto popular trends that don't align with your core essence, which can dilute your unique purpose and identity.

- **Failure to notice evolving community needs:** Regularly reassess whether your strategies authentically respond to changing community needs and conditions, which ensures relevance and impact.

By carefully navigating these dangers, you can effectively integrate strategic authenticity into your strategic thinking, ensuring decisions resonate with both core values and practical realities of the sector.

🛠 Capability-building tools & techniques

Here are some ways to skill up in strategic authenticity:

- **Narrative intelligence workshops:** One of the most potent ways to cultivate strategic authenticity is through the mastery of narrative intelligence. These workshops train individuals and organisations to weave authenticity into their stories, both internal and external. Understanding how to authentically represent oneself or an organisation sets the foundation for strategic decision-making.

- **Scenario planning with authenticity filters:** Typical scenario planning is about preparing for various future states. But when each scenario is evaluated through the lens of your core mission and values, it evolves into a tool for strategic authenticity. Courses and facilitators specialising in this nuanced approach are increasingly available.

- **Critical reflection journals:** A tool common in executive leadership programs, these journals serve as platforms for consistent reflection. Instead of focusing solely on performance metrics, these reflections also ask deep questions about alignment with core values and mission, prompting regular authentic check-ins.

- **Ethical decision-making models:** There are specific frameworks designed to make ethics an integral part of decision-making. Skilling up in these models helps embed authenticity into every strategy, from team management to product development.

- **Digital footprint analysis tools:** In an age of big data, understanding your organisation's digital footprint can provide invaluable insights into how authentically your brand is perceived. Specialised software can evaluate this and help recalibrate strategies to be more in alignment with core values.

- **Peer consultancy circles:** This collaborative approach gathers professionals from various sectors to offer insights and guidance on each other's strategic plans and challenges. The diversity of perspectives, coupled with a commitment to authenticity, can enrich one's approach to strategy. Many professional networks are now formalising this as a structured method for skill-building.

Remember, the key to strategic authenticity is embedding it into the organisational culture and individual mindset, rather than treating it as an add-on. These methods offer more than just skill-building; they offer a transformative lens through which all decisions are made.

Q **CASE STUDY**
SUSTAINABLE IMPACT

Let's talk about a nonprofit organisation deeply rooted in combating homelessness. In an industry replete with well-meaning initiatives, this nonprofit stood out by committing to strategic authenticity. Its mission wasn't just about throwing money at the problem or providing temporary relief; it was about systemic change. It engaged with government agencies, other nonprofits and the private sector, but maintained an uncompromising focus on its core objective—creating long-term housing solutions.

The Board and the team didn't see their mission as a

series of projects, but as an ongoing strategy woven into the fabric of the community. Every decision, whether it was fundraising, advocacy or program development, was aligned with this mission. The result? Not just another band-aid solution, but a series of groundbreaking community housing models that are now being replicated across the country.

By keeping its strategy tethered to its authentic purpose, the organisation galvanised community support like never before, raised substantial funds and, most importantly, moved the needle in a social problem it aimed to solve. Its success serves as a master class in strategic authenticity for the nonprofit sector.

📖 Resources and references

Some deep dive references for you:

Brown, Brené. *Dare to Lead: Brave Work. Tough Conversations. Whole Hearts.* New York: Random House, 2018.

Duckworth, Angela. *Grit: The Power of Passion and Perseverance.* New York: Scribner, 2016.

Duhigg, Charles. *The Power of Habit: Why We Do What We Do in Life and Business.* New York: Random House, 2012.

Godin, Seth. *This is Marketing: You Can't Be Seen Until You Learn to See.* New York: Portfolio, 2018.

Grant, Adam. *Originals: How Non-Conformists Move the World.* New York: Viking, 2016.

Ibarra, Herminia. *Act Like a Leader, Think Like a Leader.*
    Boston: Harvard Business Review Press, 2015.

Newport, Cal. *Deep Work: Rules for Focused Success in a
    Distracted World.* New York: Grand Central Publishing,
    2016.

Pink, Daniel H. *Drive: The Surprising Truth About What
    Motivates Us.* New York: Riverhead Books, 2009.

Ries, Eric. *The Lean Startup: How Today's Entrepreneurs Use
    Continuous Innovation to Create Radically Successful
    Businesses.* New York: Crown Business, 2011.

Sinek, Simon. *Start with Why: How Great Leaders Inspire
    Everyone to Take Action.* New York: Penguin Books, 2009.

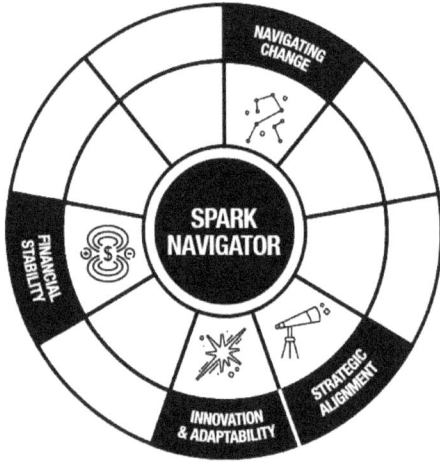

NAVIGATING CHANGE (CH)

STRATEGIC ALIGNMENT (AL)

INNOVATION & ADAPTABILITY (IN)

FINANCIAL STABILITY (FS)

ASPIRATIONAL THINKING

'ASPIRATIONAL THINKING' is a phrase that can elicit eye rolls as quickly as it can fire up a room. When sparking your strategic brain, this is not about setting lofty goals; this is about giving yourself (and your workplace) permission to recalibrate how you think so you can reach for outcomes that, at first glance, seem unreachable. So, let's deep dive, shall we?

Navigating the cosmos requires more than just technology and science; it demands a mindset that's as boundless as the universe itself—aspirational thinking. Imagine a consortium of global space agencies aspiring not just to land humans on Mars, but to make the Red Planet our second home. While the goal sounds audacious, it's this very aspiration that sets the strategic course.

This kind of thinking challenges us to ask, 'What if Mars could truly be a sustainable habitat for humanity?' Such an aspiration compels researchers, engineers and leaders to go beyond the confines of conventional space exploration. It drives innovation in terraforming, harnessing renewable energy from Martian resources, and finding biotechnological solutions for long-term human survival. It's not just about surviving; it's about thriving.

Our strategies shift from mere exploratory missions to comprehensive colonisation blueprints. It's this aspirational vision that could one day see Mars bustling with life, echoing Earth's vibrancy. In the vast expanse of space, where infinite possibilities await, aspirational thinking reminds us that our ambitions are only limited by the scope of our dreams. After all, in the quest for the stars, we move beyond new frontiers and expand what we believe to be possible.

Aspirational thinking is not about mere dreams or fantasies; it's about elevating your perspective, setting your sights on goals that might seem audacious but hold the promise of profound impact. It's the marriage of ambition with purpose. This form of thinking challenges the status quo, urging you to ask 'What is?', but also 'What could be?' It's about extending the boundaries of possibility, envisioning futures that are not mere extensions of the present, but transformative leaps forward.

For those engaged in strategy, especially in the nonprofit and for-purpose sectors, aspirational thinking serves as a compass, pointing towards a future that might seem distant but is profoundly compelling.

It's the mindset that allowed visionaries to dream of a world without polio, a society where education is accessible to all, or a planet that thrives in ecological harmony.

A quote that comes to mind, which underscores the essence of this concept, is from Robert F. Kennedy: 'Some men see things as they are, and ask why. I dream of things that never were, and ask why not.'

🕔 When to use this Spark

Aspirational thinking is most potent during the vision- and mission-crafting stages of strategic planning. When laying down the foundational ethos of an organisation or charting out a long-term strategy, aspirations guide the way, ensuring that the journey is not just about mitigating challenges, but about reaching new summits.

Aspirational thinking shines brightest when you're at a crossroads, where the future is uncertain and the stakes are high. It offers a light, ensuring that even amid ambiguity, the vision remains clear and visible.

📝 How to use this Spark

To cultivate aspirational thinking in your approach to strategic planning, focus on these developmental steps:

1   **Cultivate a visionary mindset:** Begin by nurturing a mindset that envisions bold, transformative futures. It's about allowing yourself to dream big and think beyond the constraints of current circumstances when addressing a strategic matter.

2   **Learn from visionary leaders:** Think about your strategic matter or problem and research whether the thought processes of visionary leaders can help ... understand how they conceive and pursue lofty ideas. This involves reading their works, listening to their talks and analysing their strategies.

3   **Practise backward planning:** Write down the outcome from Step 1 and practise the technique of backward planning—mapping the steps back from this idea to the present.

4   **Set stretch goals:** Challenge yourself to see this map littered with stretch goals that push your limits and expand your thinking.

5   **Reflect and adapt:** Consistently reflect on your progress towards these aspirations, remaining flexible and ready to adapt your strategies as needed.

By integrating these steps into your strategic thinking practice, you will develop a more aspirational approach, aiming not just for what is achievable in the short term, but for what can transform and elevate your work in the long run.

☑ The outcomes of using this Spark

For a nonprofit, practical outcomes from integrating aspirational thinking into strategic thinking include:

- **Enhanced inventiveness:** When we think high, we often see new things. We tend to give ourselves permission to relax a whole lot of boundaries. The boundaries, while right and real, can close us off to 'what if' opportunities. If we can just focus our minds on inventing boundary crushers, then new solutions for addressing social issues will emerge.

- **Increased motivation:** Clear and aspirational thinking boosts motivation among volunteers and staff—both intrinsic and extrinsic. Aligning these two forms of motivation is a key precondition to engagement.

- **Deeper engagement:** Hope lives in each of us. Aspirational thinking helps us tap into hope and create a common binding thread. People want to deliver their dream and this is just as true for service delivery people as it is for donors. A compelling aspirational idea can attract and retain motivated people with the hope of transformative impact.

- **More impact:** Setting ambitious goals gets our blood pumping and invites us to strive for more. It is proven to drive effort towards more significant and sustained change.

- **Valuable partnerships:** Bold aspirations can unearth new and different partnerships; ones that can really expand our field of opportunity, leading to collaborations with like-minded organisations and amplifying impact.

- **Greater sustainability:** Aspirational planning typically forces us to ask some of the 'Okay, but how do we fund this?' type questions and should bake in pencil sketch options for sustainability.

These outcomes help the nonprofit not just to meet current needs, but to forge a path towards a more impactful and transformative future.

⚠ Dangers to beware of

In developing aspirational thinking for strategic planning, you should be mindful of several potential pitfalls:

- **Unrealistic ambitions:** While it's important to aim high, aspirational goals must still be grounded in reality.

- **Head in the clouds:** Don't neglect the organisation's immediate and operational needs.

- **Demotivation:** Extremely ambitious goals can be daunting. It's crucial to set intermediate, achievable targets to maintain motivation and momentum.

- **Too much stretch:** Aspirational thinking should not lead to overstretching resources. It's essential to balance ambition with available resources and capabilities.

- **Zero followers:** It's important to ensure that stakeholders understand and support the aspirational vision to avoid resistance or confusion.

By staying vigilant about these challenges, you can ensure that aspirational thinking enriches your strategic planning process, driving you towards impactful and achievable long-term goals.

⚒ Capability-building tools & techniques

For those seeking to inculcate aspirational thinking into their strategic palette, consider these psychological tools:

- **Affirmative inquiry:** This approach to problem-solving focuses on the strengths at hand and takes a positive approach to leveraging these strengths. It has four main stages—Discovery, Dream, Design and Delivery. This approach takes us from asking, 'What's the best of what is?' to saying, 'We can activate this solution this way.'

- **Visualisation:** Aspirational thinking helps us with our dreams and goals and its companion, visualisation, helps us imagine how the rubber will hit the road. In this way it is a key ingredient to ensuring aspiration does not float off into the stratosphere.

- **Growth mindset:** We have heard this term a lot and I was a little reluctant to use it here. That said, if we can change the way we see the world into a view that features growth and abundance, then the nature of our aspirational thinking will also grow—which can only be good when solving complex social and other problems.

- **Narrative crafting:** Sometimes our aspirations feel like hunches or intuition. The ability to translate this feeling into a story is critical to bring others on the journey.

When you look at this list you will see more than just tools—you will see suggestions of changed ways of processing. Some of these suggestions take time and are a pursuit in and of themselves. Thinking strategically is not a sprint.

CASE STUDY
AN ASPIRATIONAL ODYSSEY

In the vibrant city of Melbourne, OceanGuardians, a nonprofit dedicated to marine conservation, found itself grappling with declining donor engagement and public apathy towards oceanic issues. While its efforts were commendable, the vision—'Save the Australian coral reefs—seemed too parochial. Although vital, this goal resonated only with a niche audience.

Upon engaging in some strategic workshops, heavily inspired by the concepts I champion, OceanGuardians was introduced to aspirational thinking. Instead of merely conserving, it envisioned: 'Transforming the world's oceans into thriving marine utopias by 2050'.

This aspirational shift was transformative. Its programs transcended mere conservation. It initiated global marine educational drives, collaborated with international marine conservationists, and leveraged technology to rejuvenate marine ecosystems.

The results? Astounding. OceanGuardians' donor base tripled within two years, with partnerships forged across five continents. Its vision became a rallying cry, turning a local nonprofit into a global marine conservation leader. Aspirational thinking not only rejuvenated its strategy, but elevated its impact on a global scale.

📖 Resources and references

Here are some resources to inspire your aspirational thinking:

Carr, Nicholas. *The Shallows: What the Internet Is Doing to Our Brains*. W.W. Norton & Company, 2010.

Case, Steve. *The Third Wave: An Entrepreneur's Vision of the Future*. Simon & Schuster, 2016.

Cooperrider, D., & Whitney, D. *Appreciative Inquiry*. Berrett-Koehler, 2005.

Dweck, C. *Mindset: The New Psychology of Success*. Random House, 2006.

Harari, Yuval Noah. *Homo Deus: A Brief History of Tomorrow*. Vintage, 2017.

Kaku, Michio. *The Future of the Mind: The Scientific Quest to Understand, Enhance, and Empower the Mind*. Doubleday, 2014.

Lanier, Jaron. *Ten Arguments for Deleting Your Social Media Accounts Right Now*. Henry Holt and Co., 2018.

Newport, Cal. *Deep Work: Rules for Focused Success in a Distracted World*. Grand Central Publishing, 2016.

Ries, Eric. *The Lean Startup: How Today's Entrepreneurs Use Continuous Innovation to Create Radically Successful Businesses*. Crown Business, 2011.

Russell, Bertrand. *A History of Western Philosophy*. Simon &
    Schuster, 1972.
Taleb, Nassim Nicholas. *The Black Swan: The Impact of the
    Highly Improbable*. New York: Random House, 2007.

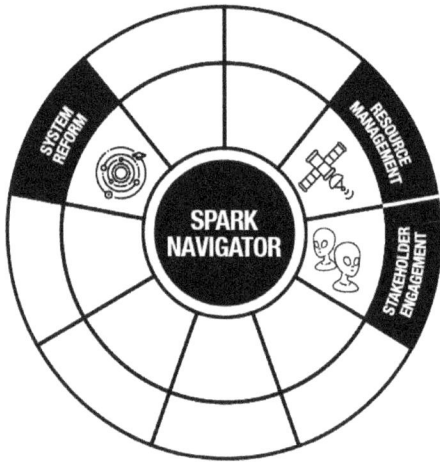

RESOURCE MANAGEMENT (RE)

STAKEHOLDER ENGAGEMENT (ST)

SYSTEM REFORM (SR)

STAKEHOLDER ENGAGEMENT

IF I had a dollar for every time someone dropped the term 'stakeholder engagement' as if it were some sort of magic incantation to solve all challenges ...

Stakeholder engagement is so much more than asking lots of people for their opinions. It is the orchestrated effort to communicate with and involve people who have an interest or stake in your organisation's activities and outcomes. It's not a PR exercise, nor is it merely consultation; it's a genuine, two-way dialogue that informs, influences and ultimately enhances strategic decision-making.

If you're a fan of space exploration, like me, think of stakeholder engagement as assembling your mission control for a trip to Mars. This isn't a solo mission, mate; it's a collective voyage requiring a galaxy of expertise—from rocket scientists and engineers to nutritionists and psychologists. Each stakeholder brings a unique piece of the puzzle, ensuring not only a successful liftoff but a sustainable Martian colony.

Now, let's say NASA wants to send the first humans to Mars. It would be ludicrous, not to mention irresponsible, for NASA to craft a mission strategy with-out engaging a broad spectrum of stakeholders. It would consult with international space agencies, private tech firms, ethical and environmental organisations, and, yes, even future Martian colonists if it could. The mission's success depends on it. These stakeholders provide insights into mission-critical elements, be it fuel efficiency, life-support systems, or the social ramifications of colonisation. By engaging them, NASA can build a more robust, foolproof strategy, one that not only reaches Mars but also lays the foundation for sustainable life there.

In this universe or any other, the principle remains the same: a well-guided strategy is a collective endeavour. And just as you wouldn't embark on an interplanetary mission without thorough preparation and all-around input, your strategic planning should never be an insular exercise.

I love the ethos of Neami and Flourish, two organisations in the psychosocial field that excel in engaging lived experience stakeholders. It's in their very DNA. One step in their approach is to build capability in those you want to engage with to get the most out of the engagement. So they undertake training and coaching with lived experience stakeholders on how to give terrifically valuable feedback on the services they want and need.

Yes, it's true! Something many people either don't think about or forget is that getting value from engaging stakeholders means you have to educate them on how to provide their insights. Think about it. You want the best insight from them so that your strategic thinking can be the best … so help them to help you!

Now, don't get me wrong. I understand that it's tempting to forge ahead with your strategic vision, powered solely by internal expertise. After all, 'He who is best prepared can best serve his moment of inspiration,' as Samuel Taylor Coleridge said. But an internally focused strategy is like trying to navigate through the Amazon using an antiquarian sketch— you might have some idea of where you want to go, but no idea of where you are going subject to the current.

When to use this Spark

In the analysis phase, stakeholder perspectives can provide critical insights into your organisation's weaknesses and opportunities. During the option-generation phase, they can contribute diverse ideas that might not emerge from an internal brainstorming session. And when it comes to implementation, stakeholders can become valuable allies, helping to mitigate risks and champion the strategy.

Whenever your strategy involves direct impact on stakeholders, it makes sense to use this Spark. Understanding them also means that you will want to engage when, due to significant changes to external environments, stakeholder engagement becomes non-negotiable. It's also critical when the stakes are high in terms of social, environmental or community impact. Engaging stakeholders isn't just best practice; it's the only practice if you aim to develop a resilient, responsive and, most importantly, responsible strategy.

How to use this Spark

To develop the skill of stakeholder engagement in strategic thinking, follow these steps:

1 **Identify who:** Identify the people you need to engage with on the matter you are thinking about. These may include donors, beneficiaries, staff, volunteers, partners and community members.

2 **Utilise empathy maps:** Walk in stakeholders' shoes using empathy maps to best understand what they seek, and the pains they experience in getting what they seek.

3 **Create a lineup:** Pick the elements of the empathy map that your thinking is trying to address. This involves balancing diverse needs with your purpose.

4 **Plan to engage on common ground:** Create tailored strategies for engaging different stakeholder groups on these areas of commonality in a way that works for them. This might involve regular updates, collaborative projects or feedback sessions.

5 **Cross-check their capability:** Ask yourself if these stakeholders have the ability to give you what you need or if they need to be upskilled.

6 **Regularly conduct joint reviews:** Sit together regularly to review progress.

7 **Build long-term relationships:** Social problems have many sides and take time to solve. My guess is you will be working with them for a long time.

By methodically developing these steps, stakeholder engagement becomes an integral and skilful part of your strategic thinking, ensuring your strategies are informed, supported and enriched by the perspectives of those you serve and collaborate with.

☑ The outcomes of using this Spark

So, what can you expect to get out of this Spark? How is it going to help you? The outcomes are:

- **Legitimate strategy:** It is my view that strategy should be based on value creation. The best way to craft value creation is to engage the consumers of this value. I think the view that Steve Jobs put forward around 'build it and they will come' is rubbish. It's just a different form of value identification and creation. Great engagement will lead to great strategy.

- **Improved trust:** Engaging with consumers and lived experience in the development of strategy (and subsequent products and services) is a highway to trust, as people will feel engaged with your work and feel heard in the process.

- **Greater sustainability:** Products and services that meet a need and deliver value have longer lifecycles—which in the social sector means predictable income streams over time.

- **Improved predictive capability:** The diverse viewpoints offer a 360-degree perspective, helping you to identify potential pitfalls and unforeseen opportunities.

- **Better stakeholder relationships:** This approach builds relationships, turning stakeholders into advocates who have a vested interest in your success.

⚠️ Dangers to beware of

In developing stakeholder engagement skills for strategic thinking, you will need to be cautious of several factors:

- **Overlooking minority voices:** Ensure that all stakeholder groups, especially those less vocal, are represented and their views are considered. The loudest voices often volunteer their opinions.

- **Failure to balance diverse interests:** Be wary of the challenge in balancing the conflicting interests of different stakeholders without compromising the organisation's purpose.

- **Miscommunication:** Pay attention to clear and effective communication to avoid misunderstandings or misinterpretations of intentions or actions.

- **Engagement fatigue:** Be mindful not to overburden stakeholders with constant requests for input, which can lead to disengagement.

- **Assumed consensus:** Avoid assuming that agreement from a few stakeholders represents the views of all.

- **Lack of authenticity:** Ensure that engagement is genuine and not just a tick-box exercise, as this can erode trust.

- **Resource misallocation:** Monitor the resources dedicated to stakeholder engagement to ensure they are proportionate and effective.

By being aware of these challenges, you can enhance the efficacy of stakeholder engagement in your strategic thinking, ensuring it's inclusive, balanced, and genuinely beneficial for your organisation and stakeholders.

Capability-building tools & techniques

Here are some techniques to help you develop this skill:

- **Ethnographic shadowing:** This immersive approach involves closely observing stakeholders in their natural environments, documenting their daily routines, interactions and decision-making processes. Ethnographic shadowing goes beyond standard interviews and surveys, offering real-world context that can be invaluable for understanding stakeholder perspectives.

- **Sentiment analysis algorithms:** Utilise machine learning and natural language processing to scan stakeholder communications—like emails, social media posts or transcripts of meetings—for emotional tone and content. This advanced method helps organisations identify stakeholder sentiment shifts in real-time, allowing for immediate and nuanced strategy adjustments.

- **Blockchain for transparent decision-making:** Incorporate blockchain technology to allow stakeholders to directly input into decision-making processes. A blockchain could record stakeholders' opinions and ideas, ensuring transparency and immutability. It can make the consultative process more transparent and verifiable, thus fostering trust and better engagement.

- **Virtual reality scenarios:** Develop immersive VR experiences that put stakeholders directly into scenarios that the organisation faces. It can be a powerful way to elicit authentic reactions and facilitate more profound, empathetic understanding among stakeholders and decision-makers alike.

- **Interactive data visualisation:** Employ advanced data visualisation tools that allow stakeholders to manipulate variables and instantly see potential outcomes. This not only democratises data but also makes complex issues easier to understand, allowing stakeholders to engage on a deeper level.

- **Dark web scouring tools:** As unconventional as it sounds, tracking stakeholder sentiments on less accessible parts of the internet could provide uncensored insights into their true feelings. Specialised software can monitor mentions and discussions related to your organisation or industry, providing a fuller picture of stakeholder sentiment.

Each of these methods has the potential to radically reshape the conventional wisdom around stakeholder engagement. They allow for a more nuanced, multifaceted understanding of stakeholder dynamics, which is indispensable in today's complex environment.

CASE STUDY
LIFELINE AUSTRALIA'S TRANSFORMATION

When Lifeline Australia realised its suicide prevention hotlines were inundated but its resources were stretched, it knew it was time to optimise its strategy. It wasn't interested in the run-of-the-mill 'more money' solution. No, it sought something transformative. Enter stakeholder engagement.

Lifeline took the radical step of involving not just its Board members but also hotline volunteers, social workers, healthcare professionals and, most crucially, the callers themselves—those in dire need of its service. Together, they dissected the pain points of the existing system. They found that callers often required varied support beyond immediate suicide prevention. The social workers shed light on the cyclical nature of mental health disorders, while healthcare professionals recommended a multi-tier support system.

The result was staggering. Lifeline implemented a more comprehensive service, including follow-up calls and resource referrals. Efficiency increased by thirty per cent, but, more importantly, the new service model resulted in a twenty-five per cent decline in repeat emergency calls. In this instance, the stakes couldn't have been higher. By including everyone who held a stake, Lifeline didn't just evolve; it revolutionised its impact.

📖 Resources and references

These references should provide a robust foundation for understanding stakeholder engagement, especially as it relates to strategic thinking:

Ayuso, Silvia, Antonio Argandoña, and Heike Brühl. 'Responsible Corporate Governance: Towards a Stakeholder Board of Directors?' *Corporate Ownership and Control* 2, no. 4 (2005): 9-19.

Andriof, Jörg, and Sandra Waddock. 'Unfolding Stakeholder Engagement'. In *Unfolding Stakeholder Thinking*, 19-42. Sheffield: Greenleaf Publishing, 2002.

Bryson, John M. *Strategic Planning for Public and Nonprofit Organizations*. 5th ed. Hoboken, NJ: Wiley, 2018.

Freeman, R. Edward. 'Stakeholder Theory of the Modern Corporation'. *Business Ethics*, edited by W. Michael Hoffman, Robert E. Frederick, and Mark S. Schwartz, 38-48. Boston: McGraw-Hill, 2001.

Frooman, Jeff. 'Stakeholder Influence Strategies: The Roles of Structural and Demographic Determinants'. *Business & Society* 39, no. 1 (2000): 1-19.

Mainardes, Emerson Wagner, Helena Alves, and Mario Raposo. 'Stakeholder Theory: Issues to Resolve'. *Management Decision* 49, no. 2 (2011): 226-252.

Mitchell, Ronald K., Bradley R. Agle, and Donna J. Wood. 'Toward a Theory of Stakeholder Identification and Salience: Defining the Principle of Who and What Really Counts'. *Academy of Management Review* 22, no. 4 (1997): 853-886.

Post, James E., Lee E. Preston, and Sybille Sachs. 'Managing the Extended Enterprise: The New Stakeholder View'. *California Management Review* 45, no. 1 (2002): 6-28.

Savage, Grant T., Timothy W. Nix, Charles J. Whitehead, and Joseph D. Blair. 'Strategies for Assessing and Managing Organizational Stakeholders'. *Academy of Management Executive* 5, no. 2 (1991): 61-75.

Tapscott, Don, and Alex Tapscott. *Blockchain Revolution: How the Technology Behind Bitcoin Is Changing Money, Business, and the World*. New York: Penguin, 2016.

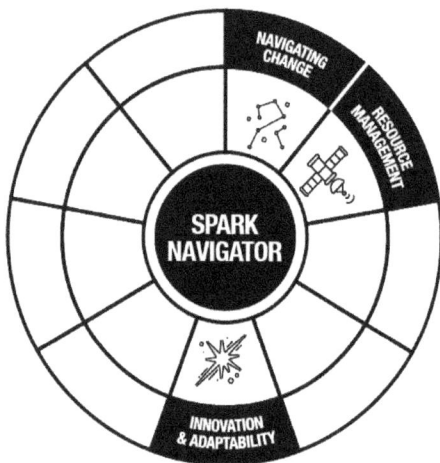

NAVIGATING CHANGE (CH)

RESOURCE MANAGEMENT (RE)

INNOVATION & ADAPTABILITY (IN)

ADAPTIVE CREATIVITY

ADAPTIVE CREATIVITY, at its core, is the interplay of flexibility and innovation in response to ever-shifting challenges and environments. Renowned strategist and philosopher, Sun Tzu, once remarked, 'In the midst of chaos, there is also opportunity.' This encapsulates the essence of adaptive creativity. It's about navigating the often-tumultuous waters of change and uncertainty with a spirit of invention.

In the annals of science fiction, there's a tale of a distant future when humanity has ventured deep into the cosmos and settled on a planet named Veridia. This new world, unlike Earth, has three suns, resulting in unpredictable daylight cycles and extreme climatic variations. Building a sustainable habitat here was no small feat. For the settlers of Veridia, traditional Earth-centric approaches were futile. So they employed adaptive creativity.

Their architects designed dynamic shelters that could morph based on the suns' positions, offering shade and light precisely when needed. Agriculturalists, faced with irregular solar patterns, genetically crafted crops that could photosynthesise optimally, regardless of the suns' unpredictable cycles. But the most ingenious was their creation of the 'ChronoSphere', a technological marvel that adjusted time perception for its inhabitants. Instead of adhering to a twenty-four-hour cycle, days inside this sphere expanded or contracted, aligning seamlessly with Veridia's erratic days and nights. This adaptive solution ensured that humans maintained their circadian rhythms, even if the world outside marched to a different beat.

This fictional journey into Veridia echoes the heart of adaptive creativity. In a setting where old rules no longer apply and challenges are novel, it is this blend of adaptability and innovation that paves the way for survival and progress. So, as we strategise for our real-world for-purpose missions, may we channel the spirit of Veridia's pioneers, always ready to creatively adapt to whatever new horizons we face.

As we delve deeper into this Spark, I hope you can see adaptive creativity as an evolution of the traditional creative process. Instead of purely focusing on originality and the invention of a 'monolith' solution that will stand the test of time, adaptive creativity emphasises resilience, responsiveness, and the ability to continuously reshape strategies based on fresh insights and changing circumstances. In a world dominated by rapid technological advances and unpredictable societal shifts, the ability to adapt creatively isn't just a strategic advantage—it's a necessity.

To further understand its significance, consider the words of Albert Einstein: 'The measure of intelligence is the ability to change.'

When to use this Spark

Adaptive creativity is particularly potent during times of uncertainty, when timelines are tight, or when facing complex, multifaceted challenges. In such scenarios, conventional solutions or rigid strategies can fall short. An adaptive creative approach allows for fluidity, ensuring that strategies remain relevant and effective even as external factors change.

Adaptive creativity ensures that strategies are not just novel, but also malleable. As the ancient Chinese text *Tao Te Ching* suggests, 'The wise adapt themselves to circumstances, as water moulds itself to the pitcher.'

How to use this Spark

To implement this Spark in strategic thinking, I tend to broadly follow these steps. Having said this, what you will find here are not so much rigid steps as ingredients or mindsets to prepare you. You will probably also see the steps as a blend of creative thinking, scenario development and continuous review:

1   **Deploy your petri dish:** Set up conditions for this Spark to thrive. These conditions include:

   a   **A curious mindset:** Encourage constant curiosity. This involves asking questions, exploring new ideas and staying open to different perspectives.

   b   **A diverse pool of experiences and knowledge:** Actively seek experiences and knowledge outside of the usual scope of thinking on this matter or problem. This could mean exploring different industries, cultures or academic fields to broaden the thinking horizon.

   c   **An experimentation-welcoming environment:** Foster an environment where creative experimentation is valued. This includes trying out new approaches and being open to unconventional solutions.

   d   **A 'failure rocks' mindset:** Embrace failures as learning opportunities. Analyse what didn't work and why, using these insights to inform future creative endeavours.

   e   **Regular brainstorming sessions:** Conduct regular brainstorming sessions with the team, encouraging the free flow of ideas without immediate judgement or criticism.

   f   **Being well-informed on trends:** Keep abreast of emerging trends and patterns within your sector and beyond, using this information to inspire adaptive creative strategies.

2   **Reflect and adapt:** As this Spark is about adaptation, it is inherently reactive or responsive to actual or forecast change. You need a way to be alerted of impending change (refer to *When to use this Spark*). Regularly reflect on the outcomes of creative strategies and be prepared to adapt them based on feedback and changing circumstances.

3   **Go back to basics:** When your trigger (Step 2) is flicked, ask why the existing thinking would still hold and be willing to go to the whiteboard.

4   **Know what you need to win:** Reset your success criteria and re-engage your thinking about how to make this happen.

5   **Invent and innovate:** Get into the fun bit of creativity. Invent totally new thinking or innovate existing thinking.

6   **Stress-test against known evidence and experience.**

By implementing these quasi steps, adaptive creativity becomes a key component of my strategic thinking process, enabling more dynamic, innovative and responsive strategy development.

☑ The outcomes of using this Spark

Incorporating adaptive creativity into a nonprofit's strategic thinking can lead to several practical outcomes:

- **Innovative program solutions:** Mastering the art of adaptive creativity allows you to develop more innovative and effective programs that better meet the evolving needs of beneficiaries by allowing you to pivot and experiment as you develop your thinking.

- **Improved resource utilisation:** We all know that time cannot be recovered and is one of the most valuable assets a nonprofit has. We also all know that things change—all the time. Given the sheer percentage of your total expenses committed to human resources, applied liberally, this Spark will help you find creative ways to maximise limited resources. This in turn leads to greater efficiency and impact.

- **Stronger community engagement:** By using adaptive creativity to listen and respond to community needs, novel approaches can be formulated. These will, in turn, help you to engage the community, forge deeper connections and build interesting funding support.

- **Increased organisational agility:** Embedding adaptive creativity means an organisation is better equipped to respond swiftly and effectively to changing external environments or challenges.

- **Diverse stakeholder appeal:** This approach leads to creative and dynamic initiatives, therefore attracting a broader range of supporters and volunteers.

- **Sustainable growth:** Encouraging adaptive creativity fosters a culture of innovation that drives long-term sustainability and growth.

By embracing adaptive creativity, a nonprofit can enhance its responsiveness, effectiveness and appeal, which are crucial for achieving its mission in a dynamic and ever-changing landscape.

⚠ Dangers to beware of

When integrating adaptive creativity into a nonprofit's strategic thinking, it's important to be cautious of:

- **Misalignment with mission:** Ensure creative strategies align with the core mission and don't stray from the organisation's primary objectives.

- **Over-innovation:** Avoid becoming so focused on innovation that it leads to neglecting proven methods or strategies that already work effectively.

- **Resource imbalance:** Be careful not to allocate excessive resources to new, creative initiatives at the expense of essential and proven, ongoing programs.

- **Stakeholder resistance:** Prepare for potential resistance from stakeholders who may be more comfortable with traditional approaches. I find this resistance more with Boards than with executives.

- **Favouring novelty over quality:** Ensure that the pursuit of creativity doesn't compromise the quality or effectiveness of programs and services.

- **Unsuitable/absent risk management:** While encouraging creativity, be mindful of risks and have contingency plans in place.

- **Inappropriate evaluation methods:** Creative strategies might require unique or modified evaluation methods to accurately assess their impact and effectiveness.

By being aware of these factors, adaptive creativity can be harnessed effectively, ensuring that it enhances rather than complicates the strategic planning process.

🛠️ Capability-building tools & techniques

Here are some ways to develop this muscle:

- **Design thinking workshops:** Engaging in hands-on design thinking workshops can give you an immersive experience in adaptive creativity. These workshops teach you how to approach problems from various angles and develop iterative solutions, equipping you to be both creative and adaptable. Several global firms offer remote workshops, so geography is no barrier.

- **Neuroscience courses:** Understanding the brain's role in creativity can significantly amplify your ability to think adaptively. Online platforms offer neuroscience courses focused on creativity. These courses delve into the psychological and biological mechanisms behind creative thinking, offering insights you can apply in a strategic setting.

- **Cross-disciplinary training:** Consider taking courses or attending seminars that are outside your field but still related to decision-making and strategy. This could include anything from economics to behavioural psychology. The idea is to diversify your thinking patterns, which will make you more adaptable and creative in your strategic approaches.

- **AI and data analytics tools:** Get comfortable using advanced data analytics and AI tools that can assist in decision-making. These tools can take creative strategies and adapt them in real-time based on incoming data, effectively training you to think more adaptively. Platforms like Coursera and Udacity offer courses in data science and AI tailored for business decision-making.

- **Gamification techniques:** Learning through gaming isn't just for kids. Several apps use gamification to teach complex subjects, including strategic thinking and problem-solving. Apps like Lumosity or even strategy games like *Civilization* can help sharpen your adaptive creativity skills in an engaging way.

- **Peer learning groups:** Join or form a peer learning group focused on adaptive creativity. Such groups can be either online or in-person and allow for a diversified form of learning. Members can share resources, offer feedback on real-world projects, and even collaborate on experimental approaches to problems. Platforms like Meetup or even Linke-dIn can help you find or initiate such groups.

Dedicated focus on these six modern methods can exponentially elevate your ability to think creatively yet adaptively, thereby honing your strategic prowess to cutting-edge levels. Whether it's absorbing the cerebral intricacies behind creativity or playing a strategy game, your route to mastering adaptive creativity is a multifaceted journey worth embarking on.

CASE STUDY
MISSIONGEN

MissionGen Australia, a nonprofit in Melbourne, exemplified the power of adaptive creativity to address evolving societal needs and technological advancements. Traditional strategies were falling short so the leadership, experienced in strategic facilitation, embraced innovation and adaptability. Initially, their youth-focused educational and vocational programs were losing engagement. Implementing adaptive creativity, they started by listening to the youths' growing interest in digital media and technology.

Transforming its program, MissionGen introduced digital media production, as well as coding and entrepreneurship courses, and continuously refined them based on feedback. This initiative included guest lecturers from Melbourne's tech scene and partnerships with local tech firms for internships. The result was a dramatic increase in engagement and success, with many participants advancing in tech-focused studies or securing jobs.

This journey highlighted that innovation must align with the evolving needs and aspirations of beneficiaries. It wasn't just the introduction of a digital program that marked its success, but the cultivation of a culture valuing adaptability and evolution. MissionGen Australia's story is an inspiration for the for-purpose sector, demonstrating that in a constantly changing world, strategies must also evolve. Its success reaffirms my belief in the transformative power of adaptive creativity, where strategy is a dynamic dance requiring adaptability and creative spirit to achieve meaningful, lasting impact.

📖 Resources and references

Now, if you're hungry for edgy resources, check out the podcast *The Accidental Creative*, which specifically focuses on adaptability in creative roles. These are also worth looking at:

Chandra, Priya, and Kai Huang. *Emergent Tech and the Art of Adapting: A Deep Dive into Creative Evolution*. Brisbane: TechFuture Publications, 2022.

Donovan, Lyle J. *Rethinking Creativity: The Age of Adaptive Solutions*. Melbourne: Australian Innovation Press, 2021.

Foster, Elijah, and Melina D'Souza. 'Beyond Innovation: The Role of Adaptive Creativity in Sustainable Business Models'. *Green Enterprise Review* 5, no. 3 (2020): 56-75.

Holloway, Freya. 'Navigating Crises: Adaptive Creativity in the Face of Global Challenges'. *Leadership and Strategy Today* 28, no. 6 (2020): 33-50.

Matthews, Isla, and Ashton Parke. 'Adaptive Creativity in a Digital World: Navigating the Unknown'. *Journal of Modern Strategy* 34, no. 2 (2022): 45-62.

Morelli, Luca. 'Culture and Adaptive Creativity: A Cross-Continental Analysis'. *Global Strategy Journal* 10, no. 1 (2021): 88-107.

Nyugen, Linh. 'The Digital Renaissance: How Adaptive Creativity is Reshaping Industries'. In *Trends in Digital Transformation*, edited by Jamal K. Singh, 192-210. Adelaide: South Coast Publishers, 2021.

Patel, Anaya, and Rafael Torres. *Virtual Realities and the Surge of Adaptive Creativity*. Perth: Western Insight Press, 2022.

Vega, Rodrigo. 'The Neuroscience of Flexibility: How Brain Plasticity Influences Adaptive Creativity'. *Brain and Innovation Quarterly* 12, no. 4 (2021): 13-29.

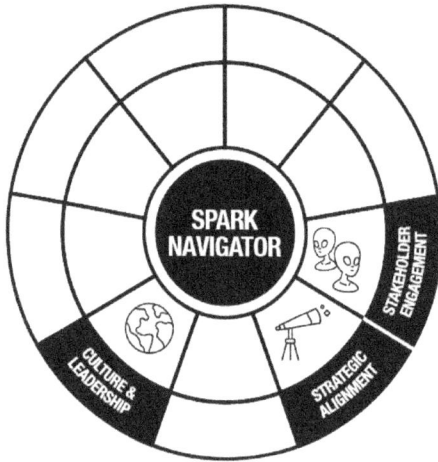

STAKEHOLDER ENGAGEMENT (ST)

STRATEGIC ALIGNMENT (AL)

CULTURE & LEADERSHIP (CL)

PURPOSEFUL
THINKING

DID YOU know that the origins of the word 'purpose' are French and have the connotation of *intentionality* and *ambition*? For purposeful thinking you need both forms—a higher goal and ambition. The first sets direction, the second ignites action.

Let's venture into the realm of outer space, shall we? Imagine you're at the helm of a spacecraft embarking on a mission to Mars. You've got all the technical know-how, from trajectory computations to the specifics of Martian soil composition. But why are you going to Mars in the first place? That 'why'—the answer to that question—is your purpose.

Having a purpose in this context is like deciding not just to reach Mars, but to do so in a way that benefits humankind. Maybe it's a quest for alternate living spaces as Earth reaches its carrying capacity, or perhaps you're seeking to unlock the secrets of life's existence elsewhere in the cosmos. That core purpose will guide every strategic decision you make. It will determine what equipment you take, which crew members are selected, and even how you'll engage with Earthlings following you from afar.

Your spacecraft will undoubtedly encounter obstacles—meteor showers, equipment failures, or unanticipated gravitational pulls. But because you and your crew are rooted in your purpose, these will become problems to solve, not reasons to quit. The strategic moves you make aren't just about dodging asteroids; they're steps towards fulfilling a grander vision. So, in the quest for Mars, just like in strategic thinking, remember: it's not just the 'how' or the 'what'; it's the 'why' that charts the course to truly transformative journeys.

Purposeful thinking, or what some might relegate to the realm of 'being intentional', has been frequently underestimated when discussing strategic thinking. But don't be fooled; this is no superficial concept. Purposeful thinking is the bedrock of meaningful strategy. It's like DNA—individual genes may be small, but together they determine the life, health and longevity of the organism.

Here's the crux. Many organisations see themselves as 'purposeful' because they have a social or environmental mission or problem to solve. Yet they meander along without a compass, relying on faith, a charismatic leader or their past goals and hoping that they're broadly going in the right direction.

Without purposeful thinking they may resist change or be captivated by whatever is shiny and new.

Jumping from one project to the next, they're prisoners of happenstance rather than architects of destiny. But when you incorporate purposeful thinking into your strategic outlook, you develop a laser focus on your end goals. You delineate not just a roadmap, but also the 'why' behind each point on that map.

At the end of the day, people may not remember exactly what you did, or how you did it, but they will always remember why you did it. So, let's not just go through the motions. Let's be deliberate, let's be purposeful, and let's achieve something extraordinary.

🕐 When to use this Spark

When is purposeful thinking most beneficial in strategic planning? The answer is twofold: at the inception of the strategic process and throughout its execution. At inception, purposeful thinking helps align your strategic objectives with your core mission. It banishes redundancy and keeps you from barking up the wrong tree. Throughout execution, it works as a sieve—filtering out distractions and accentuating your focus.

And why is purposeful thinking often superior to other concepts like analytical or tactical thinking? Simply put, without a clearly defined purpose, analytics are just numbers and tactics are mere motions. Aristotle wasn't joking when he said, 'The whole is greater than the sum of its parts.'

How to use this Spark

To incorporate purposeful thinking into your strategies, employ these steps:

1   **Define your core purpose:** Start by clearly articulating the fundamental purpose of the organisation. This involves understanding your mission and the core values that drive you.

2   **Align goals with purpose:** Ensure that all strategic goals are directly aligned with this core purpose. Each objective should reflect and advance your primary mission.

3   **Adopt purpose-driven decision-making:** When faced with strategic choices, consistently ask how each decision aligns with and furthers your purpose. This becomes a guiding principle for all decision-making.

4   **Communicate the purpose:** Effectively communicate this core purpose across the organisation. Ensure every team member understands and is committed to this central mission.

5   **Integrate your purpose into organisational culture:** Foster a culture where purposeful thinking is valued and practised at all levels. Encourage teams to regularly consider the purpose in their daily tasks and decisions.

6   **Regularly review alignment:** Continuously review strategies and operations to ensure they stay aligned with the core purpose, making adjustments as needed.

7   **Measure impact based on purpose:** Develop metrics to measure how well your strategies and actions are fulfilling your organisational purpose.

By methodically practising these steps, purposeful thinking becomes deeply ingrained in your strategic approach, ensuring that every decision and action taken is consciously aligned with your core mission and long-term vision.

☑ The outcomes of using this Spark

The outcomes of using this Spark are myriad, but all essential. Integrating purposeful thinking into strategic thinking brings many benefits:

- **Enhanced mission alignment:** Purposeful thinking ensures all strategies and activities are closely aligned with the nonprofit's core mission, enhancing alignment and, in turn, overall mission effectiveness.

- **Increased donor confidence:** Setting your intention and embedding it clearly into your strategic thinking demonstrates a clear and consistent commitment to the mission. This consistency and clarity fosters confidence among donors and stakeholders.

• **Improved program relevance and impact:** Employing this Spark leads to the development of programs and initiatives that are more relevant and impactful to the communities served. A note on this ... far too often I see mission creep as organisations seek more funds. This Spark is great for curtailing this mission creep.

• **Stronger organisational identity:** Purposeful thinking helps to establish a clearer organisational identity and value proposition, which is important for branding and positioning.

• **Greater employee and volunteer engagement:** When their work is clearly connected to the nonprofit's purpose, staff and volunteers become more deeply engaged and committed.

• **Strategic decision-making efficiency:** Purposeful thinking streamlines decision-making processes, as choices are evaluated based on their contribution to the core mission.

• **Long-term sustainability:** By consistently focusing efforts on what truly matters to its mission and vision, an organisation will enhance its sustainability. It will do this because its focus will ensure resources are not wasted or diverted to mission creep activities. It will also do this because funders will see the Theory of Change embedded in your thinking, which calls out the straight line between their dollars and the impact produced.

By adopting purposeful thinking, a nonprofit ensures its strategies are not just effective, but also resonate deeply with its mission, stakeholders and the communities it serves.

⚠ Dangers to beware of

Every Spark in this book comes with certain dangers. In applying purposeful thinking to strategic planning, it's important to be aware of potential pitfalls:

- **Rigid thinking:** Avoid becoming so focused on the mission that it leads to inflexibility, which in turn can lead to missing out on innovative opportunities or necessary adaptations.

- **Narrow focus:** Be cautious of concentrating solely on the mission to the extent that it overlooks broader impacts or external factors.

- **Stakeholder misalignment:** Ensure that, while being mission-focused, the needs and expectations of diverse stakeholders are not neglected.

- **Overlooking operational realities:** Balance mission-driven strategies with practical operational considerations, ensuring the organisation remains viable and effective.

- **Resistance to change:** Be aware of potential resistance from within the organisation to changes that align with the purpose but require new ways of working.

- **Poor communication:** Clearly communicate the purpose and its implications to avoid misunderstandings or misinterpretations among staff, volunteers and stakeholders.

By being mindful of these factors, purposeful thinking can be more effectively integrated into strategic planning, ensuring it enhances decision-making and guides the organisation towards fulfilling its mission effectively and sustainably.

⚒ Capability-building tools & techniques

Once you have the basic process under control, you can continue to build your skill at incorporating purposeful thinking when creating strategy. Here are some tools to get you and your team going:

- **Core values exercise:** Sometimes, the purpose is a bit fuzzy because it's mixed up with a lot of other good but non-essential things. A core values exercise can help filter out the noise. Get your team together and list out all the values you think are important. Then, begin the hard task of cutting that list down to the most critical few. These core values often point directly to your core purpose.

- **Simon Sinek's 'golden circle':** This is a tool for organisations to define their purpose (Why?), how they do what they do (How?), and what exactly it is that they do (What?). By answering these in a structured manner, one can gain clarity on the overarching purpose.

- **Purpose alignment matrix:** Create a matrix where one axis lists your key activities and the other axis lists your organisational objectives and social impact goals. The intersections will help you see where you are, or are not, aligned with your purpose.

- **Stakeholder interviews:** Sometimes an external perspective can provide valuable insight. Conducting interviews with key stakeholders can offer a clearer understanding of how your actions align with your intended purpose, and may help to redefine that purpose in more actionable terms.

- **Vision boards:** An underutilised tool in a business setting, a vision board can make abstract concepts tangible. Whether using an actual board with cut-outs or a digital app, place on it images, quotes, metrics, or anything else that resonates with what you feel your purpose to be. Refer to this regularly and adjust as necessary.

- **Daily intention setting:** Start each day by setting a clear intention. It could be as simple as a sentence or a phrase that encapsulates what you aim to achieve or how you want to conduct yourself. This act can bring a surprising level of clarity and focus, helping you align your activities with your overarching purpose.

- **Time blocking for purposeful actions:** Allocate specific blocks of time for tasks that serve your intentions. If your intention is to engage more deeply with stakeholders, for example, block out two hours every week solely for that purpose. No emails, no distractions, just undivided focus on fulfilling that part of your purpose.

- **Decision filter:** Create a one-pager that includes key elements of your purpose and strategic goals. Use this as a filter for decision-making. Whenever a new opportunity or challenge arises, pass it through this filter first to see if it aligns with your purpose.

- **Mindful meetings:** Begin every internal meeting with a brief statement of its purpose and what you intend to achieve by the end. This aligns everyone's focus and enables more purposeful discussion. If the meeting diverges, anyone in the room has permission to bring it back to its stated purpose.

- **The 'five whys' technique:** Originally part of lean manufacturing, this technique involves asking 'Why?' five times in succession to drill down into the root cause of an issue or the core reason behind an activity. This can be incredibly enlightening for ensuring that your actions are aligned with your intentions and long-term objectives.

By embedding these tools into your regular strategic routines, you're not just setting an intention; you're living it in each action and decision you make. This focused approach ensures that intentionality isn't a buzzword but an actual operational asset, integral to your strategy and organisational DNA.

⌕ CASE STUDY
FOOD FOR ALL

To further understand the benefits of purposeful thinking, let's look at how it works in the real world. When Food for All, a nonprofit organisation combating hunger in urban communities, took a step back to reconsider its purpose, an incredible transformation began. For years, it was involved in just food distribution. However, after adopting a purposeful thinking approach, it asked itself the golden question: 'Why are we doing this?'

Its strategic planning underwent an overhaul. The newfound purpose was no longer just about handing out food, but enabling self-sufficiency in communities. Every program, every initiative, had to line up with this purpose. It wasn't long before its reach expanded into educational workshops on sustainable farming and financial literacy.

Within two years, the number of people empowered to grow their food tripled. Financial donations rose by forty per cent, and volunteer engagement increased because people were more attracted to a clearly articulated purpose.

📖 Resources and references

Here are some muscle-building deep dive references for you. I've selected these works for their focus on self-awareness, intentional decision-making and effective strategic thinking; all critical elements for anyone keen to employ a purposeful approach in their strategy and daily life.

Brown, Brené. *Dare to Lead: Brave Work. Tough Conversations. Whole Hearts.* Random House, 2018.

Clear, James. *Atomic Habits: An Easy & Proven Way to Build Good Habits & Break Bad Ones.* Avery, 2018.

Covey, Stephen R. *The 7 Habits of Highly Effective People: Powerful Lessons in Personal Change.* Simon & Schuster, 1989.

Duhigg, Charles. *The Power of Habit: Why We Do What We Do in Life and Business.* Random House, 2014.

Grant, Adam. *Originals: How Non-Conformists Move the World.* Viking, 2016.

Heath, Chip, and Dan Heath. *Switch: How to Change Things When Change Is Hard.* Currency, 2010.

Ibarra, Herminia. *Act Like a Leader, Think Like a Leader.* Harvard Business Review Press, 2015.

Newport, Cal. *Deep Work: Rules for Focused Success in a Distracted World.* Grand Central Publishing, 2016.

Sinek, Simon. *Start with Why: How Great Leaders Inspire Everyone to Take Action.* Portfolio, 2009.

NAVIGATING CHANGE (CH)

INNOVATION & ADAPTABILITY (IN)

FINANCIAL STABILITY (FS)

SYSTEM REFORM (SR)

RISK MANAGEMENT (RI)

ENVIRONMENTAL AWARENESS

YES, ENVIRONMENTAL awareness is the age-old practice of knowing what's happening around you. And there's a lot to know…

Imagine you're building your own space mission. You've got a destination—a far-off galaxy you want to explore. You wouldn't simply thrust your spacecraft into the void and hope for the best. First, you'd put the power of environmental awareness to work. This isn't just about checking the weather in space. It's about understanding cosmic winds, nebula densities, asteroid fields and the laws of interstellar politics. Dynamically—as you travel.

Consider the gravitational pulls of celestial bodies, how they interact in orbital dances that could either speed up your journey or hurl you into a black hole. This is your competitive landscape. And let's not forget the cosmic red tape—the treaties and universal laws you need to adhere to in this boundless frontier.

Environmental awareness in strategic thinking is like being the astronomer, the flight engineer and the cosmic lawyer, all in one. You've got the telescope, the spacecraft blueprints and the legal documents spread before you. You're not just charting a course—you're anticipating every challenge and opportunity you might encounter. And why? Because the stakes are more than high; they're cosmic. It's not a task for the faint-hearted or the unprepared. So, fire up your engines, but never stop scanning the stars.

Now let's head back to Earth and go a bit deeper to see how this works in the real world. Your awareness should span three altitudes of control:

1. **Sphere of control:** Typically, this means understanding what is going on inside you and your workplace. This is the world where you can change anything and everything. This is often called the micro world.

2. **Sphere of influence:** Usually your sector or industry. Here you can't control things, but you sure can influence them. This is often called the meso world.

3. **Sphere of interest:** This is the world you can't control or influence. Here you can only anticipate and respond. This is generally called the macro world.

Awareness in strategic thinking is often focused on the macro world and uses tools such as PESTEL (political, economic, social, technological, environmental and legal). The meso environment has used tools such as Porter's five forces, codesign with lived experience, and value proposition development. The micro environment is teased apart with business models, operating models and cultural models.

This Spark is not new nor innovative, but it is a stalwart of your strategic thinking. It helps you anticipate trends and forecast disruptions, and allows for agile, responsive strategic planning. Unlike environmental awareness, it's not just ecological. It scans every facet of the environment—political, social, economic, technological—and informs strategy accordingly.

⏱ When to use this Spark

When should you use this concept in strategic thinking? I think this is part of your weekly routine. I set aside Fridays for this type of work. Conveniently, Friday lets me grab a bite with my network and deep dive into meaty things they are seeing too.

This concept is an enabler for most of the other Sparks. It helps us set the context for the rest of our strategic thinking and rule ideas in or out. 'The essence of strategy is choosing what not to do,' notes Michael Porter. When you are completely in tune with your environment, you not only choose what to do but also what pitfalls to deftly avoid.

How to use this Spark

To develop environmental awareness in strategic thinking, you can follow these steps:

1 **Enable continuous external monitoring:** Set up the information sources, subscriptions and time in your diary to regularly monitor these three environments. Did you know some of the most successful thinkers spend about three hours a day reading and talking to people about the environment?!

2 **Connect with stakeholders:** Establish a vibrant network of stakeholders, including beneficiaries, donors and community members, to gain insights on environmental changes impacting them.

3 **Connect with cross-sector entities:** Engage in collaborations with organisations outside your mesh environment to broaden understanding of environmental factors and their implications.

4 **Perform regular scenario analysis:** Regularly conduct scenario analysis to anticipate how different environmental changes could impact your strategic goals and operations.

5 **Incorporate insight into strategic review:** Integrate environmental insights into regular strategic reviews, ensuring your strategy remains relevant and responsive.

6   **Conduct risk assessment and management:** Continuously assess risks associated with environmental changes and develop strategies to mitigate them.

7   **Conduct staff training and development:** Encourage and facilitate staff training on environmental trends and their relevance to your work.

By methodically practising these steps, environmental awareness becomes a core component of your strategic thinking, enabling you to anticipate, adapt to, and leverage external changes effectively.

The outcomes of using this Spark

Integrating environmental awareness into your strategic thinking leads to several practical outcomes:

- **Proactive adaptation:** Increased environmental awareness enhances an organisation's ability to anticipate and adapt to external changes, ensuring strategies remain relevant and effective. This is strategy 101, really.

- **Improved risk management:** Consciously building environmental awareness helps an organisation to identify and mitigate risks arising from environmental factors, which in turn protects it from potential adverse impacts. Again, 101.

- **Increased relevance and impact:** Employing this Spark creates strategies and programs that are more aligned with current societal needs and trends, increasing their relevance and impact. Further, this will help the nonprofit 'trim' what it does and cut off any misaligned or outdated programs and expenses.

- **Stronger stakeholder relationships:** Environmental awareness leads to a deeper understanding of the changing environments that stakeholders operate in, which in turn leads to stronger relationships and more effective collaboration.

- **Enhanced funding opportunities:** Becoming more aware of the environment creates the ability to identify and leverage new funding opportunities that arise from environmental changes.

- **Greater organisational resilience:** The organisation's resilience is enhanced in the face of external shifts and challenges when greater environmental awareness is in place.

By adopting environmental awareness in strategic planning, a for-purpose workplace becomes more adaptive, responsive and effective in achieving its mission in a dynamic external environment.

⚠ Dangers to beware of

When incorporating environmental awareness into strategic thinking, watch out for these pitfalls:

- **Information overload:** Ouch, my brain hurts! Be cautious of becoming overwhelmed by the vast amount of external information, which can lead to analysis paralysis. Set your informational 'field of play' and stray only occasionally...

  (May I segue a little here? Your brain takes in so much data every second that you rely on it to subconsciously filter out what you don't need (avoiding overwhelm). But it doesn't forget this other stuff. This other stuff is processed and accessed by what seems to you to be intuition. Your intuition will guide you on straying from your field of play—listen to it!)

- **Biased interpretation:** Watch for biases in interpreting external data and trends, ensuring a balanced and objective understanding. Call a friend!

- **Being overly reactive:** Avoid being overly reactive to environmental changes; focus instead on proactive strategies that anticipate future shifts.

- **Neglecting internal alignment:** Ensure that external awareness does not overshadow the need for internal alignment with the organisation's mission and capabilities.

- **Stakeholder misalignment:** Be aware of potential misalignments between external changes and stakeholder expectations or needs. You may be out in front and need to bring others up to your speed.

- **Inappropriate resource allocation:** Monitor the allocation of resources towards environmental monitoring and analysis to ensure it's proportional and effective.

By being aware of these factors, environmental awareness can be effectively integrated into strategic thinking, enhancing an organisation's responsiveness and strategic efficacy without compromising its core mission and values.

✂ Capability-building tools & techniques

Yes, environmental awareness takes effort, but, when wielded effectively, it doesn't just guide strategy; it shapes destiny. Here are some ways to beef up your environmental awareness:

- **Environmental scanning software:** There are various tools available that can provide real-time updates on trends, news and shifts within your sector or general environment. Having a dashboard that integrates information can help make sense of the external environment faster.

- **Competitive intelligence services:** Specialised firms offer this as a service, collecting data on competitors and broader market trends. This can serve as a shortcut to gaining comprehensive insights.

- **Participatory workshops:** Encourage open dialogue within the organisation where team members can share their observations and insights regarding the external environment. The collective intelligence of the group can often spot opportunities and threats that individuals miss.

- **Public and private data mining:** Learn how to scrape and interpret data from public sources like government publications and private databases. This statistical data can serve as the backbone of your environmental understanding, helping you recognise trends and make predictions.

- **Sentiment analysis tools:** Use AI-driven sentiment analysis to gauge public opinion on social issues, political shifts or consumer preferences that could impact your strategic objectives.

- **Scenario-planning software:** Advanced software can help simulate various future scenarios based on current environmental data. This can be extremely useful for understanding the possible outcomes of different strategic choices.

- **Trend analysis platforms:** Tools like Google Trends or industry-specific analytics platforms can offer insights into what is gaining attention. This can help you prepare for what's coming next.

- **Stakeholder-mapping applications:** Visualising the network of stakeholders, from vendors to local communities to policymakers, can highlight areas that need more focus for maintaining a stable external environment.

- **Podcasts and webinars:** Industry-specific discussions can be a goldmine for the latest thoughts and concerns about environmental issues relevant to your field.

CASE STUDY
THE ASTOUNDING TURNAROUND OF SHELTERMATES

At ShelterMates, an Aussie nonprofit focused on providing housing for the homeless, the team was well-versed in the art of 'doing good', but they were floundering when it came to long-term planning. Enter the concept of environmental awareness. Instead of looking solely at their internal capabilities, they embarked on a broad environmental scan.

They looked at property markets, economic forecasts, even climate reports—yes, don't snigger. They wanted to know if more extreme weather events would increase demand for shelters. This deep dive allowed ShelterMates to identify partnership opportunities with construction firms looking for CSR activities, and even predict gentrification trends to secure properties in 'up and coming' areas. The results? A forty per cent increase in shelters within a year, a swell in donations by twenty-two per cent, and a partnership with a leading construction firm. This isn't wizardry; it's what happens when you wield the power of environmental awareness in your strategic toolkit.

Environmental awareness provides the 'why' and the 'how'—why certain strategies would be more impactful and how to go about executing them in the current climate.

📖 Resources and references

Each of these sources delves into different aspects of environmental awareness and its crucial role in strategic thinking and planning. They provide theoretical frameworks, practical case studies, and empirical evidence to guide you in assimilating this concept into your strategic toolkit.

Bansal, Pratima, and Andrew J. Hoffman, eds. *The Oxford Handbook of Business and the Natural Environment*. Oxford University Press, 2012.

Epstein, Marc J. *Making Sustainability Work: Best Practices in Managing and Measuring Corporate Social, Environmental and Economic Impacts*. Berrett-Koehler Publishers, 2008.

Gladwin, Thomas N., James J. Kennelly, and Tara-Shelomith Krause. 'Shifting Paradigms for Sustainable Development: Implications for Management Theory and Research'. *Academy of Management Review* 20, no. 4 (1995): 874-907.

Hawken, Paul. *The Ecology of Commerce: A Declaration of Sustainability*. HarperCollins, 1994.

Hart, Stuart L. 'A Natural-Resource-Based View of the Firm'. *Academy of Management Review* 20, no. 4 (1995): 986-1014.

Porter, Michael E., and Claas van der Linde. 'Green and Competitive: Ending the Stalemate'. *Harvard Business Review*, September-October 1995.

Senge, Peter M. *The Fifth Discipline: The Art & Practice of the Learning Organization*. Currency, 2006.

Shrivastava, Paul. 'The Role of Corporations in Achieving
    Ecological Sustainability'. *Academy of Management Review*
    20, no. 4 (1995): 936-960.

Starik, Mark, and Gordon P. Rands. 'Weaving an Integrated
    Web: Multilevel and Multisystem Perspectives of
    Ecologically Sustainable Organizations'. *Academy of*
    Management Review 20, no. 4 (1995): 908-935.

Stead, W. Edward, and Jean Garner Stead. *Management for a*
    Small Planet. SAGE Publications, 1992.

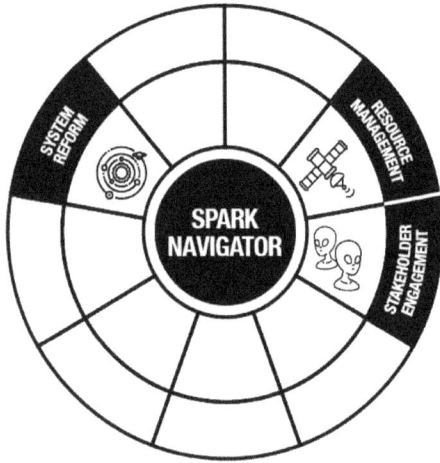

RESOURCE MANAGEMENT (RE)

STAKEHOLDER ENGAGEMENT (ST)

SYSTEM REFORM (SR)

PARTNERSHIPS

PARTNERSHIPS—THEY ARE a fundamental in both the profit and nonprofit sector. And you know what they are. But do you understand partnerships in a strategic sense? Let's examine their critical importance by once again looking skywards.

Ah, outer space—the final frontier. It's a realm that offers unparalleled examples of partnerships in action. Picture, if you will, the Mars rover. While it may have 'NASA' or 'ESA' emblazoned on the hardware, don't be fooled; this is an international symphony of minds and resources. It's not just a single nation pointing a rocket at a red dot in the sky; it's physicists, engineers and scientists from around the globe collaborating to reach a single destination. Each country brings its unique specialisation to the table, be it advanced robotics, cutting-edge software or uncharted theories on life-support systems. This strategic alliance not only helps to share hefty costs; it pools collective wisdom to solve one of the most complex problems humanity has ever faced—interplanetary existence.

By allying, the partners involved have fast-tracked advancements, mitigated colossal risks and exponentially multiplied the potential impacts of their mission. Imagine if just one country took this on. Sure, it might make some headway, but at what cost, and how many decades later? This example underscores the core lesson: partnerships don't just enable us to do more; they enable us to achieve the unthinkable. It's the epitome of strategic collaboration, offering a cosmic lesson for us all.

This might sound like tough love—because it is! You can't solve social problems or deliver your purpose on your own. Start reframing your thinking so that you ask, at every turn, how you can partner to increase the chance of success or amplify your impact.

I guess the Spark here is not the age-old 'partnering' chestnut, but rather a call for you to embed partnering as you think about every strategic issue— maybe even extend it.

I remember a former CEO of a large mental health service provider once quipping, 'You only partner when you are too small to do it yourself.' Wow, how they got that wrong!

Right here and now, forget the age-old mindset of going it alone; today's complex problems require complex solutions, which are best constructed through collaborative efforts.

Partnerships extend the boundaries of your resources, infusing fresh perspectives, skills and assets into your strategic idea—especially partnerships with those that might do your work better than you do!

🕐 When to use this Spark

Partnership works when the costs (or loss of impact) of not partnering outweigh the costs of collaboration. This can occur in scenarios requiring expertise beyond your core competencies or when a social issue extends beyond your organisation's direct influence. For instance, if you're an NGO focused on education, but realise the core issue extends to, say, family stability or income inequality, a partnership with organisations addressing those sectors becomes not just viable but crucial.

When the conversation turns to scale or systemic change, a singular approach typically reveals its limitations. Partnerships fill these gaps, offering a manifold increase in the collective capabilities, including everything from funding and human resources to distribution networks. In a world enamoured with the idea of 'innovation', remember this: innovation isn't merely technological; it's also structural. Partnerships provide the framework for this sort of structural innovation, allowing for more adaptive, resilient strategies that are more than the sum of their parts.

How to use this Spark

To develop the skill of forging effective partnerships in strategic thinking, you can follow these steps:

1 **Burn partnership into your brain:** Just for a few months, as you sit to consider a strategic matter, consciously ask yourself: 'Could partnering be more efficient, effective or simply better in this case?'

2 **Identify potential partners:** Start identifying organisations and entities whose missions, values and strategic goals align with yours. This includes both within and outside your immediate sector.

3 **Assess complementarity:** Evaluate how potential partners complement your strengths and weaknesses in relation to the idea. Look for synergies in resources, expertise and networks.

4 **Establish clear objectives:** Define clear objectives that the partnership can bring to the strategic thinking or idea.

5 **Engage in open dialogue:** Initiate conversations with potential partners around the idea at hand. Learn and teach together. Discuss mutual goals, expectations and the value each party brings to the table.

My goal is to get partnerships into your pre-frontal cortex so that you consider them reflexively. Once that's done, standard partnership development techniques can take over.

☑ The outcomes of using this Spark

Let's talk outcomes and benefits. A well-strategised partnership amplifies the reach and impact of your efforts, often accelerating the timeline towards your goals. Incorporating strategic partnerships into a non-profit's planning yields several practical outcomes:

- **Expanded reach and impact:** Collaborations can extend the reach of programs and services, amplifying an organisation's impact in the community.

- **Resource optimisation:** Partnerships often lead to shared resources, reducing costs and increasing efficiency in achieving mutual goals.

- **Enhanced program diversity:** Collaborations can bring in new perspectives and expertise, enriching program offerings and effectiveness.

- **Increased funding opportunities:** Joint initiatives can open up new funding avenues, including grants that favour collaborative efforts.

- **Strengthened sector influence:** Strategic alliances can enhance the organisation's influence and voice in sector-wide conversations and policy-making.

- **Improved learning and innovation:** Working with partners fosters learning and innovation, as each party brings unique ideas and approaches.

- **Greater sustainability:** Collaborative efforts can lead to more sustainable solutions and approaches, as they combine strengths and mitigate individual organisational weaknesses.

By strategically forming and leveraging partnerships, a nonprofit can significantly enhance its
operational efficiency, programmatic diversity and
overall impact in the community.

⚠ Dangers to beware of

When integrating partnerships into strategic planning, it's important to be aware of several potential
pitfalls:

- **Misalignment of missions and values:** Ensure that
  partners' missions and values align closely with
  yours to avoid potential conflicts and ensure cohesive collaboration.

- **Dependency:** Be cautious of becoming too depen-
  dent on a single partnership, which could create
  vulnerabilities.

- **Poor communication:** Effective and regular communication is vital; poor communication can lead
  to misunderstandings and ineffective collaboration.

- **Inappropriate expectations:** Clearly define and
  manage expectations from the outset to prevent
  disappointment or misalignment of objectives.

- **Misallocated resources:** Monitor the distribution
  of resources within partnerships to ensure it's balanced and aligns with agreed-upon objectives.

- **Failure to meet goals:** Regularly assess the effectiveness and impact of partnerships to ensure they are meeting strategic goals.

- **No exit strategy:** Have a clear exit strategy for the partnership, should it no longer meet its objectives or benefit the organisation.

By keeping these considerations in mind, partnerships can be effectively integrated into an organisation's strategy, enhancing its capacity to achieve broader goals and impact.

✂ Capability-building tools & techniques

Deploying these contemporary approaches challenges the status quo, using fresh tactics and technologies to turn the age-old concept of partnerships on its head, reframing it for the complex, fast-moving world we find ourselves in:

- **Leverage the gig economy:** Instead of traditional long-term commitments, try project-based partnerships that pull in freelancers or smaller companies as short-term, but highly specialised partners. This lets you tap into very specific skill sets or market opportunities quickly and flexibly.

- **Use blockchain-enabled contracts:** Make partnership contracts transparent and tamper-proof using blockchain technology. It not only adds a layer of security but speeds up processes like verification, making the partnership agile and built on mutual trust.

- **Deploy AI-powered matchmaking:** Use advanced machine learning algorithms to sift through potential partners, matching your organisation with those whose goals, values and capabilities align with yours. This data-driven approach saves time and increases the odds of a successful partnership.

- **Use open innovation platforms:** Create a digital space where potential partners can contribute ideas and projects in line with your strategic objectives. It's a way to crowdsource partnerships and co-create value.

- **Embrace social impact bonds:** For public and social sector entities, social impact bonds are a fresh way to structure partnerships that align each party around measurable outcomes. Private investors provide upfront capital and are repaid by the government, but only when agreed-upon social outcomes are achieved.

- **Employ sustainable supply chain collaborations:** Team up with companies in your supply chain to co-create more sustainable processes. Not only does this optimise costs and efficiencies, it also elevates the social responsibility profile for everyone involved.

Q CASE STUDY
THE RIVER FOUNDATION

Let me tell you about the River Foundation, a Melbourne-based nonprofit centred around local river conservation. It had noble aims, but was consistently hampered by funding issues and public awareness. Then it decided to play to its strengths and leveraged partnerships with local businesses and community organisations. What we're talking about here isn't just throwing a logo on a brochure. No, it went deeper than that. It orchestrated a comprehensive plan to partner with local schools, businesses and even governmental bodies to bring about true, long-lasting impact.

The result? A massive uptick in funding and volunteer numbers, sure, but the real win was in the results. River pollution dropped by forty per cent in two years. It was able to build sustainable programs, like local school trips for kids, to understand the importance of river conservation, which had ripple effects throughout the community. By forming strategic partnerships, the River Foundation exponentially increased its impact and sustainability.

Resources and references

I've focused on a mix of classic and cutting-edge works that delve deep into various facets of partnerships. These sources will give you a comprehensive understanding of how partnerships have evolved and where they are headed, especially in the context of strategic thinking.

Ashby, Alison, Ken Starkey, and Nicholas P. M. Waring. 'Public-Private Partnerships and the Public Good: A Review'. *Journal of Business Ethics* 161, no. 4 (2020): 665-678.

Austin, James E., and M. May Seitanidi. 'Collaborative Value Creation: A Review of Partnering Between Nonprofits and Businesses'. *Nonprofit and Voluntary Sector Quarterly* 40, no. 5 (2011): 726-758.

Brinkerhoff, Jennifer M. 'Government-Nonprofit Partnership: A Defining Framework'. *Public Administration and Development* 22, no. 1 (2002): 19-30.

Fitzgerald, Louise, and Ewan Ferlie. 'Professionals: Back to the Future?' *Human Relations* 56, no. 5 (2003): 713-739.

Gray, Barbara, and Donna J. Wood. 'Collaborative Alliances: Moving from Practice to Theory'. *The Journal of Applied Behavioral Science* 27, no. 1 (1991): 3-22.

Ingram, Helen, and Dean Mann. 'Interest Groups and Environmental Policy'. *Environmental Politics and Policy*, 1954-1994, 187-209. Washington, D.C.: CQ Press, 1995.

Kania, John, and Mark Kramer. 'Collective Impact'. *Stanford Social Innovation Review* 9, no. 1 (2011): 36-41.

Porter, Michael E., and Mark R. Kramer. 'Creating Shared Value'. *Harvard Business Review* 89, no. 1/2 (2011): 62-77.

Tapscott, Don, and Anthony D. Williams. *Blockchain Revolution: How the Technology Behind Bitcoin and Other Cryptocurrencies is Changing the World*. New York: Penguin Random House, 2018.

Vangen, Siv, and Chris Huxham. 'Enacting Leadership for
Collaborative Advantage: Dilemmas of Ideology and
Pragmatism in the Activities of Partnership Managers'.
British Journal of Management 16, no. S1 (2005): S59-S75.

.

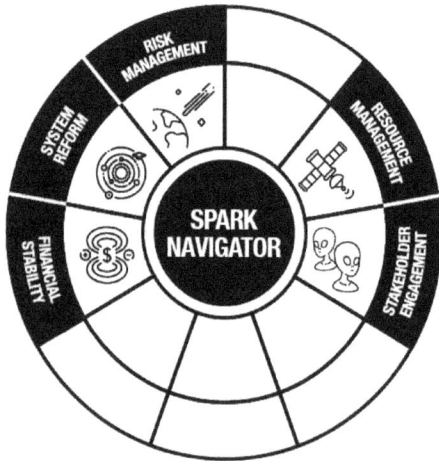

RESOURCE MANAGEMENT (RE)

STAKEHOLDER ENGAGEMENT (ST)

FINANCIAL STABILITY (FS)

SYSTEM REFORM (SR)

RISK MANAGEMENT (RI)

SYSTEMS
THINKING

SYSTEMS THINKING is the process of understanding how things influence one another within a whole. In essence, it's about seeing through chaos to discern the underlying structures that cause problems and recognising the subtle interconnections that influence one another, often in surprising ways. 'To understand is to perceive patterns,' Isaiah Berlin once noted, and this is precisely what systems thinking equips us to do.

Imagine a civilisation on a distant exoplanet facing a critical challenge: their planet's once abundant resources are depleting rapidly. Historically, each region tried to tackle this crisis independently, often leading to competitive hoarding and inefficient usage. The need of the hour? Systems thinking.

They began viewing their planet not as fragmented territories, but as an interconnected biosphere. Just as stars and planets in a galaxy influence each other through gravitational forces, every action taken in one region had cascading effects planet-wide. By acknowledging these intricate linkages, the civilisation adopted a unified approach to resource management. Technologies were shared, best practices became common knowledge, and regions that once competed now collaborated.

In this celestial backdrop, systems thinking didn't just ensure the survival of the exoplanetary civilisation; it forged a harmonious, interconnected society. Their holistic view, much like the vast interconnectedness of the universe, became the linchpin to sustainable progress and prosperity. Systems thinking, whether on Earth or in the far reaches of space, emerges as a universal solution to complex problems.

This Spark is about building the muscle that helps you see the world as an interconnected whole rather than isolated fragments. It's a massive thing to wrap your head around that makes you ask not just what's in the frame, but what the frame leaves out.

Peter Senge, author of *The Fifth Discipline*, described it eloquently: 'Systems thinking is a discipline for seeing wholes. It is a framework for seeing interrelationships rather than things, for seeing patterns of change rather than static snapshots.'

The challenges we face in our organisations and communities are seldom the result of single, isolated causes. They're systemic, and they demand a systemic perspective.

Consider the multifaceted issue of climate change. It's not just about CO_2 emissions or deforestation, but involves economic systems, political policies, consumer behaviours, technological advancements and cultural narratives. Addressing such a challenge requires understanding these interconnections and seeing the system as a whole.

🕐 When to use this Spark

While other thinking approaches might offer depth in specific areas, systems thinking stands out for its breadth. It's a vantage point from which we can appreciate both the forest and the trees, understanding not just individual elements but how they relate and coalesce into broader patterns.

Systems thinking is best used when addressing a complex issue or issues, with multiple stakeholders across multiple transactions or time horizons. Given how this describes most social issues, I like to think about this as my go-to tool when I want to develop a hypothesis to solve a social problem.

It's also great when focusing on identifying and rallying groups of stakeholders around a community or social matter.

Think complex, multi-party and multiple transactions.

📋 How to use this Spark

To develop the skill of systems thinking in strategic planning, follow these steps:

1   **Understand the concept:** Begin by thoroughly understanding what systems thinking entails—recognising patterns, interdependencies and the dynamics within complex systems.

2   **Identify key elements:** In any strategic scenario, identify all key elements—stakeholders, processes, resources—and how they interact.

3   **Map the system:** Create visual maps of these elements and their relationships to understand the broader system and potential leverage points.

4   **Analyse patterns and trends:** Look for recurring patterns and trends within the system. This can reveal underlying structures and inform more effective strategies.

5   **Consider long-term implications:** Evaluate the potential long-term impacts of strategic decisions within the system, moving beyond immediate effects.

6   **Encourage team learning:** Foster a culture of learning and exploration within the team, encouraging everyone to think in terms of systems.

7   **Apply and iterate:** Regularly apply systems thinking to strategic challenges and refine your approach based on feedback and results.

By methodically practising these steps, you will enhance your ability to apply systems thinking to your strategic planning, ensuring a more holistic, informed and effective approach to tackling complex challenges.

☑ The outcomes of using this Spark

By using systems thinking in strategic planning, we're more equipped to anticipate the ripple effects of our decisions, discerning not just immediate consequences, but those that emerge from the complicated web of interactions in the system.

Applying systems thinking to an organisation's planning results in several important benefits:

- **Enhanced understanding of complex issues:** Applying systems thinking leads to a deeper understanding of the complexities and interdependencies within an organisation's operational environment and allows it to adjust its Theory of Change from a blunt instrument to a finely nuanced scalpel.

- **More effective problem-solving:** Developing strategies that address root causes, rather than just symptoms, leads to more sustainable solutions for all involved.

- **Improved stakeholder engagement:** Thinking about the system, not just its parts, leads to better understanding and managing of the diverse needs and impacts of various stakeholders. In turn, this leads to stronger relationships and collaborations.

- **Increased operational efficiency:** Identifying and addressing systemic inefficiencies leads to more effective use of resources, both inside the organisation and across those working on the same social issue.

- **Long-term impact planning:** Systems thinking assists in creating strategies that consider long-term implications and sustainability, which ensures lasting impact.

- **Risk mitigation:** By proactively identifying and managing potential risks within the system, an organisation enhances its resilience.

- **Innovative program development:** Fostering a holistic view encourages innovative approaches to program design and delivery.

By incorporating systems thinking into strategic thinking, an organisation can achieve more nuanced understanding, efficient operations and impactful, sustainable strategies.

⚠ Dangers to beware of

In incorporating systems thinking into an organisation's strategic planning, it's important to be mindful of:

- **Over-complexity:** Avoid getting lost in the complexity of systems to the point where it hampers decision-making and action.

- **Assumption errors:** Be cautious of assumptions made in mapping and analysing systems, as they can lead to flawed conclusions.

- **Change resistance:** Prepare for potential resistance within the organisation, as systems thinking can challenge conventional approaches.

- **Imbalance between detail and big picture:** Ensure a balance between focusing on specific elements of the system and maintaining an overall perspective.

- **Inadequate time and resource investment:** Recognise that thorough systems analysis requires significant time and resources, which need to be managed effectively.

- **Unmet implementation challenges:** Be aware of the challenges in translating systems thinking into practical strategies and actions.

- **Infrequent adaptation:** Systems are dynamic, so regularly update your understanding and strategies to reflect changes in the environment.

By keeping these considerations in mind, systems thinking can be effectively integrated into strategic planning, enhancing an organisation's approach to complex problem-solving as well as taking advantage of bigger and brighter opportunities.

⚒ Capability-building tools & techniques

Developing skill in systems thinking can be done using the following methods:

- **Gaming and simulation:** Games like *Pandemic* or digital platforms like *SimCity* and *Civilization* are designed around complex systems. Playing such games can help cultivate an intuitive understanding of systems dynamics, feedback loops and emergent behaviours.

- **Ecological immersion:** Immersing oneself in nature, such as forest bathing or permaculture farming, offers a direct experience of interdependence and systems dynamics. Nature is the original complex system, and understanding its nuanced relationships can inform our understanding of man-made systems.

- **Improvisational theatre:** Engaging in improv exercises or joining an improv group can foster an appreciation for immediate feedback, adaptation and interconnected storytelling—all of which are central to systems thinking.

- **Interactive system modelling platforms:** Tools like Wolfram's SystemModeler or NetLogo allow for the creation of complex system models. They offer a more hands-on, experimental approach for those who want to build and test system models iteratively.

- **Dialectical behavioural thinking:** This method encourages looking at opposites and understanding how they can co-exist in a system. It's about reconciling and balancing seemingly conflicting views, similar to the yin-yang philosophy.

- **Cultural exchange or travel:** Engaging deeply with another culture—its norms, structures and social contracts—offers insights into alternative societal systems. This can lead to greater understanding of systems dynamics and adaptability.

CASE STUDY
OCEAN CONSERVATION TRUST

The Ocean Conservation Trust (OCT), a nonprofit committed to protecting marine ecosystems, found itself facing a conundrum. While it was deeply aware of the pressing issues threatening our oceans, there was a noticeable disconnect between its efforts and the engagement level of the wider community. Enter systems thinking. The OCT realised that merely addressing isolated problems—such as plastic pollution or overfishing—wouldn't bring about the desired change. It had to consider the ocean as a holistic system, interconnected in every sense.

Upon adopting a systems thinking approach, OCT began to map out the multifaceted relationships between different marine threats. This led it to some unexpected stakeholders, like local businesses and schools. By running workshops and educational programs that explored the broader impacts of human behaviour on marine life, the OCT demonstrated how a seemingly small action could cascade through the system and create larger challenges for marine conservation.

The results were transformative. The OCT not only amplified its impact, but also diversified its donor base and volunteer workforce. Local businesses became more eco-conscious and adapted their operations to be more sustainable, and schools integrated marine conservation into their curricula. All these seemingly disparate entities now understood their role within the larger oceanic system. The OCT's systems thinking approach had not just raised awareness, but fostered an entire community committed to safeguarding the oceans.

📖 Resources and references

Some more deep dive doses:

Booth Sweeney, Linda, and Donella Meadows. *The Systems Thinking Playbook*. Chelsea Green Publishing, 2008.

Complexity Labs. Online Courses. https://complexitylabs.io/

International Society for the Systems Sciences. https://isss.org/

Kim, Derek H. *Introduction to Systems Thinking*. Pegasus Communications, 1999.

Meadows, Donella. *Thinking in Systems: A Primer*. Chelsea Green Publishing, 2008.

Senge, Peter M. *The Fifth Discipline*. Doubleday/Currency, 1990.

Sterman, John D. *Business Dynamics: Systems Thinking and Modeling for a Complex World*. McGraw-Hill, 2000.

The Systems Thinker. Online platform. https://thesystems-thinker.com/

Wheatley, Margaret J. *Leadership and the New Science*. Berrett-Koehler, 2006.

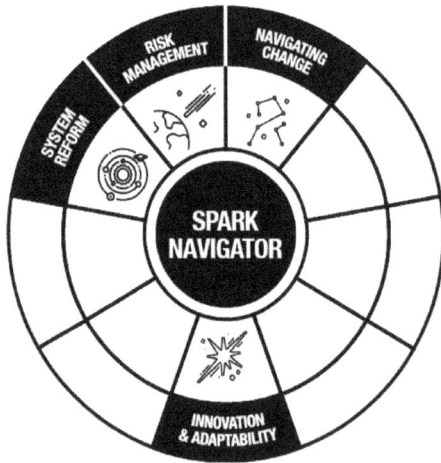

NAVIGATING CHANGE (CH)

INNOVATION & ADAPTABILITY (IN)

SYSTEM REFORM (SR)

RISK MANAGEMENT (RI)

CONCEPTUAL
BOUNDARY SPANNING

THIS SPARK holds the promise of transformative brilliance, especially when considered through the lens of the for-purpose sector. Thinking that spans conceptual boundaries will teach you how to fuse and harmonise disparate thought processes into a cohesive whole.

Similar to, but different from, pattern recognition, it uses your creative mind, and often your subconscious memory, to identify and fuse memories and new ideas from many sources.

On the vibrant planet of Avalon, nestled in the Orion Nebula, Governor Tara faced a labyrinth of interconnected challenges. Avalon, a melting pot of diverse cultures, advanced technologies and rich natural ecosystems, was at a crossroads where environmental, technological, social and economic factors converged.

Avalon's challenges encompassed the integration of rapidly advancing technologies with traditional social structures, the management of resource scarcity amid technological abundance, and the preservation of cultural heritage in an age of borderless galactisation.

Governor Tara convened a council representing a spectrum of disciplines—from environmentalists and tech innovators to sociologists, historians and economists. In their discussions, environmentalists explored the socio-cultural impacts of conservation efforts, technologists considered the ethical implications of their innovations, and historians provided insights into preserving cultural identities in rapidly changing societies.

This collaborative crucible led to the emergence of a multi-pronged strategy. It involved developing sustainable technologies that honoured Avalonian traditions, creating economic policies that fostered both technological advancement and environmental stewardship, and implementing educational programs that blended historical wisdom with modern knowledge.

Governor Tara's adept navigation through conceptual boundary spanning transformed Avalon's complex challenges into a symphony of coordinated solutions. This approach became a beacon across the Orion Nebula, showcasing how embracing complexity and integrating diverse perspectives can lead to harmonious, sustainable and forward-thinking governance.

At its heart, thinking that spans conceptual boundaries is an intellectual pilgrimage. It beckons us to venture beyond the familiar terrains of our specialised knowledge, to tap into diverse disciplines, cultures and experiences. It's about recognising the inter-connectedness of our world and drawing upon this vast web to craft strategies that resonate deeply and widely. As Albert Einstein once remarked, 'The significant problems we face cannot be solved at the same level of thinking we were at when we created them.' And it's this evolution of thought, this transcendence of conceptual barriers, that this paradigm champions.

Thinking across disciplinary boundaries is less about mere collaboration and more about synthesis. It's the art of weaving threads of knowledge from disparate fields into a cohesive tapestry that can address multifaceted challenges. This approach is imperative for those in strategic roles, as solutions crafted in isolation often fail to resonate in our interconnected world.

When to use this Spark

Boundary spanning is great when exploring new funding opportunities that require collaboration with different sectors or industries, in situations when partnering with other organisations can significantly extend the reach and effectiveness of your programs, when tackling multifaceted social problems that benefit from a multidisciplinary approach and diverse perspectives, and when pursuing invention and innovation.

How to use this Spark

To develop the skill of boundary spanning in strategic thinking, you can follow these sequential steps:

1 **Create bubbles:** Write down your problem in a big circle on a whiteboard. Around it place other circles containing the different 'areas' this problem touches. An 'area' could be things like internal structures, meso or macro environments, geographies, cohorts . . . this is a gathering, not a filtering, activity.

2 **Prioritise your bubbles:**

   a Classify your bubbles as either:

      i   Inside your workplace

      ii Related to partners and your sector/industry/social problem

      iii Remote environment

   b Redo your picture with the issue at the centre and then place three rings around your issue and label these three new rings: 'Inside', 'Partners' and 'Remote'.

   c Drop each bubble into the appropriate ring

3 **Understand intersecting domains:** Gain a deep understanding of the closest bubbles. This includes understanding the discipline or area of thought that could best be used on this bubble—the perspectives, challenges and opportunities.

4 **Build cross-boundary relationships:** Actively cultivate relationships with individuals and organisations who can share a view on, or expertise in, these bubbles. Networking, partnerships and collaborative projects are key tools here.

5 **Facilitate information exchange:** Encourage and facilitate the flow of information and ideas across these boundaries. This could involve setting up joint meetings, cross-sectoral forums or shared knowledge platforms.

6 **Develop integrative thinking:** Foster an ability to think in an integrated way, merging insights and ideas from across boundaries to inform strategic decisions.

7 **Implement and reflect:** Apply boundary-spanning strategies in your planning and operations, and regularly reflect on their effectiveness, adapting as necessary.

By methodically practising these steps, you will enhance your ability to span boundaries in your strategic thinking, which is crucial for fostering innovation, adaptability and comprehensive problem-solving.

The outcomes of using this Spark

Employing conceptual boundary spanning in strategic thinking creates these practical outcomes:

- **Broader perspectives in problem-solving:** Integrating diverse viewpoints from across boundaries leads to more comprehensive understanding of the issue, a deeper knowledge of what has been tried before and a view on creative ways to solve the problem.

- **Enhanced collaboration opportunities:** Mastering conceptual boundary spanning establishes stronger partnerships across silos and with external organisations, which increases opportunities for joint initiatives and resource sharing.

- **Innovative program development:** Fostering cross-sectoral collaborations can result in inventive and innovative program designs that blend the best of two different approaches. This blending can often serve the 'whole person' and in doing so better meet community needs.

- **Increased funding potential:** Using this method expands funding possibilities through diversified partnerships and enhanced visibility across new adjacent sectors. A new term is emerging here—'intersectional impact'.

- **Strengthened community engagement:** Spanning conceptual boundaries builds deeper connections with the community by engaging with a wider range of stakeholders and understanding their diverse needs.

- **Greater organisational influence:** These techniques will enhance a nonprofit's influence and advocacy capacity by being a connector and collaborator across various sectors.

- **Improved adaptability:** Mastering conceptual boundary spanning fosters an organisational culture that is more adaptable and responsive to changes in the external environment.

By integrating boundary spanning into strategic planning, an organisation can enhance its adaptability, innovation and overall impact in serving its mission.

⚠ Dangers to beware of

In implementing conceptual boundary spanning as a strategic thinking approach, it's crucial to be mindful of:

- **Mission drift:** Ensure that collaborations across boundaries do not lead your organisation away from its core mission and objectives.

- **Unbalanced resource allocation:** Watch for the potential overcommitment of resources to boundary-spanning activities at the expense of key internal projects.

- **Incorrect stakeholder expectations:** Be cautious of divergent expectations or objectives among different stakeholders, which can affect the success of cross-boundary initiatives.

- **Ineffective cross-cultural communication:** Pay attention to communication barriers, especially when spanning boundaries involving different cultural or organisational norms.

- **New or increased risks:** Assess and manage risks associated with new partnerships or ventures, including impacts on the organisation's reputation and credibility.

- **Loss of program integrity:** Ensure that the quality and integrity of programs are maintained when adapting them to different contexts or collaborations.

- **Loss of alignment:** Regularly evaluate the impact and effectiveness of boundary-spanning efforts to ensure they align with strategic goals and adapt as necessary.

By considering these specific factors, boundary spanning can be effectively utilised to enhance collaboration, innovation and impact in strategic thinking.

⚒ Capability-building tools & techniques

To embed this thinking into your strategic arsenal, try the following practices:

- **Humility and curiosity:** Cultivate a mindset of humility and curiosity. Recognise that no single discipline holds the monopoly on wisdom. Every field, be it sociology, technology, economics or the arts, offers unique insights, methodologies and perspectives. By approaching problems with an openness to integrate these diverse viewpoints, you pave the way for richer, more holistic solutions.

- **Continuous learning:** Engaging in continuous learning is crucial. Immerse yourself in literature, conferences or workshops outside your core expertise. Dabble in realms unfamiliar, seeking not mastery, but a foundational understanding that allows you to appreciate the nuances and contributions of other disciplines.

- **Dialogue:** Actively foster interdisciplinary dialogues. Establish forums, both formal and informal, where experts from varied domains can come together. These cross-disciplinary conversations often serve as crucibles where novel, boundary-spanning ideas are birthed.

- **Diversity in thinking:** Champion diversity, not just in terms of demographics, but also in thought. Teams that mirror the rich tapestry of disciplines are more equipped to traverse and bridge conceptual divides. They bring to the table a melange of approaches and problem-solving techniques, enhancing both the breadth and depth of strategic solutions.

- **Systems thinking:** Recognise that our world, in all its complexity, operates like an intricate system. Changes in one component often ripple across, affecting other seemingly unrelated elements. By understanding these interconnections and leveraging insights from diverse disciplines, you can craft strategies that are both impactful and resilient.

Q CASE STUDY
HARMONY OUTREACH

Harmony Outreach, a nonprofit in Australia's vibrant for-purpose sector, exemplifies the impact of multidisciplinary thinking in addressing complex community challenges. Faced with the intertwined issues of mental health and economic challenges in regional Australia, it moved beyond traditional, singular approaches. Instead of operating in silos, Harmony Outreach strategically bridged multiple disciplines.

Collaborating with psychologists, local business leaders, economists, sociologists and anthropologists, it gained comprehensive insights into the mental, economic and cultural landscapes of the communities. This cross-disciplinary approach led to the development of an integrated program that combined mental health support with skill development and entrepreneurship initiatives. Recognising the symbiotic relationship between economic empowerment and mental well-being, its strategy aimed to improve living standards while bolstering community morale.

The transformative results were evident in the renewed purpose and growth found by community members. They benefited from both mental health resources and opportunities for economic advancement, fostering a positive cycle of well-being and prosperity.

📖 Resources and references

Here is your deep dive dose:

Beinhocker, Eric D. *The Origin of Wealth: Evolution, Complexity, and the Radical Remaking of Economics*. London: Harvard Business Review Press, 2006.

Csikszentmihalyi, Mihaly. *The Systems Model of Creativity: The Collected Works of Mihaly Csikszentmihalyi*. Netherlands: Springer, 2014.

Johnson, Steven. *Where Good Ideas Come From: The Natural History of Innovation*. New York: Riverhead Books, 2010.

Klein, Julie Thompson. *Interdisciplinarity: History, Theory, and Practice*. Detroit: Wayne State University Press, 1990.

Kuhn, Thomas S. *The Structure of Scientific Revolutions*. Chicago: University of Chicago Press, 1962.

Osterwalder, Alexander, and Yves Pigneur. *Business Model Generation: A Handbook for Visionaries, Game Changers, and Challengers*. New Jersey: John Wiley & Sons, 2010.

Page, Scott E. *The Difference: How the Power of Diversity Creates Better Groups, Firms, Schools, and Societies*. New Jersey: Princeton University Press, 2007.

Ramo, Joshua Cooper. *The Seventh Sense: Power, Fortune, and Survival in the Age of Networks*. New York: Little, Brown and Co., 2016.

Snow, C.P. *The Two Cultures*. London: Cambridge University Press, 1959.

Taleb, Nassim Nicholas. *Antifragile: Things That Gain from Disorder*. New York: Random House, 2012.

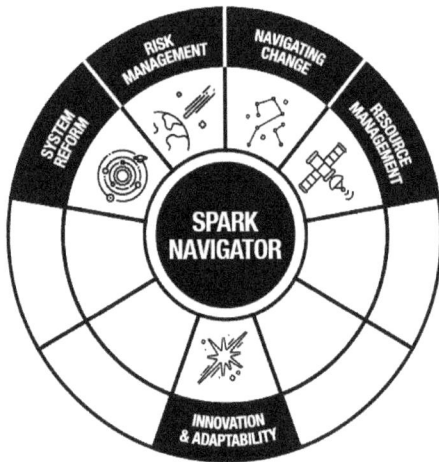

NAVIGATING CHANGE (CH)

RESOURCE MANAGEMENT (RE)

INNOVATION & ADAPTABILITY (IN)

SYSTEM REFORM (SR)

RISK MANAGEMENT (RI)

SCENARIO THINKING

SCENARIO THINKING is a systematic approach to strategy that allows organisations to explore multiple plausible futures, based on varying assumptions and drivers of change. It acknowledges the complexity and uncertainty of the future and blasts the illusion of a single forecast in favour of a spectrum of potential outcomes.

Picture this: the 'Cosmic Consortium', a conglomerate based out of Melbourne's Space Tech District, has its eyes set on interstellar colonisation. But the vastness of space, filled with infinite variables, renders traditional planning inadequate. Here, where the known universe is but a speck and the unknown stretches endlessly, scenario thinking takes on unparalleled significance.

Inspired by strategic methodologies, the consortium begins crafting scenarios for colonising Proxima Centauri b, the nearest exoplanet. One scenario envisages a lush,

Earth-like environment, primed for human settlement. Another contemplates a barren land where terraforming is essential. A third paints a picture of a planet teeming with microbial alien life, necessitating delicate first-contact protocols.

By developing these diverse scenarios, the Cosmic Consortium is not navigating blindly into the abyss; it is equipped for myriad eventualities. When its probes finally relay data from Proxima Centauri b, the consortium isn't caught off-guard. It is prepared, with blueprints in hand, to chart the next chapter of human civilisation. Through scenario thinking, it has ensured that humanity's leap into the cosmos is not a leap into the unknown but a calculated, strategic journey.

Scenario thinking helps you develop a structured way of predicting possible futures. It allows you to create vivid narratives of pathways to those futures. By using stories, you can bring others along with you as you virtually explore these potential futures, looking for opportunities and dealing with threats as you go. At its essence, scenario thinking is less about predicting the future and more about preparing for it.

(⏲) When to use this Spark

When the terrain is uncertain, when variables are many and the future seems more like a web of possibilities than a linear path, this is when scenario thinking comes to the fore. Especially in sectors undergoing rapid change or in situations where external forces (technological disruptions, geopolitical shifts, or environmental concerns) are at play, scenario thinking provides a structured way to navigate the ambiguity.

How to use this Spark

To develop the skill of scenario thinking in strategic planning, follow these steps:

1 **Identify key factors:** Start by identifying key drivers and uncertainties that could impact your organisation's future. Use the micro, mesh and macro lenses discussed in the environmental scanning Spark. This includes economic, political, social and technological factors.

2 **Develop diverse scenarios:** Based on these factors, construct a range of plausible future scenarios. These should represent different possible outcomes, from the most optimistic to the most challenging. Don't shy away from the hardest ones... 'The obstacle is the way.'—Marcus Aurelias, Rome, years ago...

3 **Analyse implications:** For each scenario, analyse the potential implications for your organisation. What would be the challenges and opportunities in each case?

4   **Undertake strategic response planning:** Develop strategic responses for each scenario. This involves considering how to adapt your strategies and operations in different future conditions.

5   **Regularly review and update:** Continuously update and refine scenarios as new information and trends emerge.

6   **Integrate into strategic planning:** Use insights from scenario thinking to inform your broader strategic planning, ensuring your strategies are resilient and adaptable.

By practising these steps, scenario thinking becomes a crucial tool in your strategic arsenal, helping you prepare for a variety of future possibilities and ensuring your organisation is ready for whatever the future holds.

☑ The outcomes of using this Spark

Integrating scenario thinking into an organisation's strategic thinking does not have to be limited to 'planning time' and can result in several beneficial outcomes:

- **Enhanced preparedness:** By imagining potential future situations, an organisation is better prepared for the impact of unforeseen challenges. It was amazing to see the difference between how two organisations responded to the pandemic—one of which picked 'pandemic' as its scenario in the previous planning round while the other didn't!

- **Informed decision-making:** Taking into account various possible future environments and their implications leads to more informed and more well-rounded strategic decisions. It also leads to a better ability to defend or validate a decision down the track.

- **Increased flexibility and resilience:** Anticipating potential future scenarios leads to improved ability to adapt to changing circumstances and enhances organisational resilience.

- **Effective risk management:** By actively charting potential future scenarios, identification and management of potential risks becomes more proactive.

- **Strategic innovation:** Considering different future possibilities encourages innovative thinking in strategy development.

- **Stakeholder confidence:** Thoroughly preparing for various futures increases confidence among stakeholders, including donors and partners.

- **Long-term sustainability:** Scenario planning encourages the development of strategies that ensure long-term sustainability and impact, regardless of changing external conditions.

By employing scenario thinking, an organisation can navigate uncertainties more effectively, ensuring its strategies are robust, adaptable and aligned with future possibilities.

⚠ Dangers to beware of

When applying scenario thinking in strategic planning, it's important to be cautious of:

- **Over-reliance on predictions:** Avoid placing too much emphasis on predicting the future; scenarios are guides, not certainties.

- **Scenario bias:** Be aware of biases in scenario creation. Ensure a range of scenarios, including less obvious or comfortable possibilities.

- **Over-complexity:** Manage the complexity inherent in scenario planning. Avoid creating so many scenarios that it becomes unmanageable or confusing.

- **Misallocation of resources:** Ensure that scenario planning doesn't consume disproportionate resources that could be used for immediate operational needs.

- **Analysis paralysis:** Avoid being so caught up in planning for various scenarios that it hampers decisive action in the present.

- **Stakeholder misunderstanding:** Clearly communicate the purpose and outcomes of scenario planning to stakeholders to prevent misunderstandings about the organisation's direction.

- **Outdated scenarios:** Keep scenarios updated and relevant; outdated scenarios can lead to misguided strategic decisions.

By being mindful of these factors, scenario thinking can be a valuable tool in strategic planning, helping the organisation to prepare for various futures without detracting from its present effectiveness.

🛠️ Capability-building tools & techniques

Here are some practical ways to develop your scenario thinking mindset:

- **Embracing uncertainty:** Regularly challenge your assumptions, understanding that the future is fluid.

- **Using diverse inputs:** Actively seek opinions from a broad spectrum of stakeholders, fostering a holistic view of potential futures.

- **Futures literacy:** Familiarise yourself with the techniques and tools used by futurists and scenario planners. This includes methodologies such as Delphi techniques, cross-impact analysis and backcasting. By practising and integrating these into your strategic thinking processes, you'll cultivate a nuanced ability to not just think about the future, but to think with it.

- **Continuous learning:** Stay updated with global trends and developments, ensuring scenarios remain relevant.

- **Reflective practice:** Regularly review past scenarios, refining the approach based on real-world outcomes.

- **Collaborative exploration:** Engage in group scenario-building exercises, leveraging collective intelligence.

🔍 CASE STUDY
FUTURECHILD FOUNDATION'S TRIUMPH

Within the bustling cityscape of Melbourne, FutureChild Foundation, a nonprofit centred on youth education and empowerment, faced a pivotal challenge. The digital revolution was altering the educational landscape at an unprecedented rate. Instead of trying to adapt reactively, the foundation, having absorbed some of the strategic paradigms I've fervently advocated, embraced scenario thinking.

Recognising the myriad possible futures in the realm of education, it charted out four distinct scenarios: a fully digitised learning ecosystem, a hybrid model of digital and traditional learning, a return to classical education methods, and a community-driven, peer-led learning model. For each scenario it developed strategic initiatives, ensuring it could pivot its approach based on emerging trends.

Its proactive approach proved visionary when the pandemic hit. While many organisations scrambled to adapt, FutureChild Foundation smoothly transitioned to its digital learning ecosystem scenario, ensuring uninterrupted education for thousands. The success of its scenario-driven strategy not only safeguarded its mission, but positioned it as a trailblazer in nonprofit educational resilience.

Resources and references

For those keen on a deep dive into the intricacies of scenario thinking, these non-mainstream resources are invaluable:

Curry, Andrew. *The Scenario Book: 30 Trend and Technology Scenarios*. Troubador Publishing Ltd, 2018.

Day, George S. *Peripheral Vision: Detecting the Weak Signals That Will Make or Break Your Company*. Harvard Business School Press, 2007.

Kahane, Adam. *Transformative Scenario Planning: Working Together to Change the Future*. Berrett-Koehler Publishers, 2012.

Lindgren, Mats. *Scenario Planning: The Link Between Future and Strategy*. Palgrave Macmillan, 2009.

Ralston, Bill. *Scenario Planning Handbook*. South-Western Cengage Learning, 2006.

Schwartz, Peter. *The Art of the Long View*. Doubleday, 1991.

Slaughter, Richard A. *The Biggest Wake Up Call in History*. Foresight International, 2010.

van der Heijden, Kees. *Scenarios: The Art of Strategic Conversation*. Wiley, 2005.

Wack, Pierre. 'Scenarios: Shooting the Rapids'. *Harvard Business Review*, 1985.

Wilkinson, Angela. *Strategic Reframing: The Oxford Scenario Planning Approach*. Oxford University Press, 2016.

CONCLUSION

AS WE reach the end of this first stage of our journey to impact, having travelled through the realms of social sector strategy, it's time to reflect on how far we have come.

You, and possibly your team, have been introduced to twenty-five transformative and highly practical 'Sparks', which together create a constellation, or framework, that I have developed and which has helped me across the twenty-five years I have been doing this work.

As I mentioned in the introduction, I had originally drafted seventy Sparks, so maybe, if enough of you get value out of this, I can publish some more! Each Spark was presented as a self-contained chapter addressing specific strategic issues pertinent to the nonprofit sector, but with relevance for the commercial and government sectors as well. These Sparks are tools for practical exploration, designed not merely for reading, but for active implementation and integration into your organisational strategies and cultures. So I hope you will put the book down long enough to put these Sparks into action. But before you do, I have ...

🔍 ONE FINAL CASE STUDY
A CEO'S TRANSFORMATIONAL JOURNEY WITH THE SPARKS

Let's delve into the story of Alex, the CEO of a nonprofit organisation dedicated to improving the lives of young people with complex or chronic mental health issues. Alex, aware of the rapidly evolving challenges within the sector, realised the necessity to revolutionise their team's strategic thinking approach. They turned to this book, seeking to ignite a transformation within their organisation, and started by uplifting their leadership team's strategic thinking capability.

Alex's rationale was that the team could only go as fast as their slowest member, so it was time to not only catch people up, but elevate them to a new level.

Alex initiated a series of bi-weekly workshops with the team, each session dedicated to unpacking and applying one of the Sparks. They began with Spark #7, Space to Think, which led the team to reconsider their current operating model. They determined that a large part of their problem was that individually and as a group they would deliver more value if they created space to solve strategic issues once and for all—even if that meant short-term service delivery drops while they got there. So, they dug into their budgets, looked for partnerships, and found ways to reduce their leadership team's hands-on work by twenty per cent. This gave them the time and space to embrace strategic thinking.

As they progressed to Spark #24, Conceptual Boundary Spanning, the team started integrating diverse methodologies and perspectives into their strategy formulation, breaking down silos and fostering a more collaborative environment. This Spark encouraged the team to look beyond traditional boundaries, considering inputs from various disciplines and sectors, thereby enriching their strategies. For example, they had heard of a disability service provider who had trained up members of the local community to act as support coordinators to their clients. Alex and the team were able to translate this practice into a youth mental healthcare setting, and in doing so not only reduced the use of expensive professionals but also fostered deeper community connection.

The journey took a technological leap forward when they deployed Spark #8, Collaborative Intelligence, which led them to harness the power of AI for enhanced environmental data analysis. This integration of technology into their strategic processes not only streamlined operations, but also opened new avenues for research and innovation.

Through this journey with the Sparks, Alex and the team underwent a transformation that transcended mere strategic development; it was a cultural shift towards innovation, adaptability and proactive thinking—key traits for any thriving nonprofit in today's complex world.

A call to action

This book is for you: leaders in the nonprofit sector. It urges you to delve deep into these Sparks, to internalise and apply them within your organisations. The nonprofit sector is undergoing rapid transformation, and the need for heightened strategic acumen has never been more pressing.

Strategic thinking, as we've seen, is not a static achievement, but a dynamic journey of continuous learning, adaptation and evolution. These Sparks are your guides on this journey, offering the necessary insights and tools to adeptly navigate the complexities and challenges of the modern nonprofit landscape.

Let's not merely plan for the future; let's strategically think our way into a better one. The Sparks presented in this book are your catalysts for change, lighting the path towards strategic excellence for your organisation. Embrace them, experiment with them, and allow them to illuminate the path towards a more innovative and impactful future for your nonprofit.

Where to from here? There's a variety of ways you can continue your strategic thinking journey with us:

- Sign up for a masterclass with George and meet other leaders while learning

- Enrol in our online course that steps through each of the Sparks

- Subscribe to and access more content, such as our interviews with leaders using these Sparks

- Sign up for group sessions for a more personalised learning experience

- Check out our blogs and podcasts

Information on all of these options is available at our website: www.sparkstrategy.com.au

BONUS MATERIAL

AS A thank-you for reading this book and engaging in its content, I'd like to give you complimentary access to some valuable companion content that will help you to further increase your strategic thinking capabilities or those of your team.

To access these resources, please visit: www. sparkstrategy.com.au/bookbonus/

There, you'll discover:

- Spark one-page printables

- Consolidated list of the resources listed in this book

- Bonus Sparks

- And more supplemental materials related to the Sparks in this book

Visit www.sparkstrategy.com.au/bookbonus/ now.

ACKNOWLEDGEMENTS

I WOULD like to acknowledge the Boonwurrung peoples of the Kulin nation as the traditional custodians of the lands on which this book was drafted. I pay my respect to elders past and present and acknowledge their vital custodianship of the lands, seas and air that we enjoy today.

To my partner, Celeste... you have inspired me with your own journey into connection and have shone a light into places I would rather not have had to think about. Both of which have been instrumental in helping this book be so much more than it was originally shaping up to be.

To my team working today at Spark Strategy, you are the tightest, nicest and most values-aligned team ever! You are making the most tremendous impact on the good people we advise. Thanks for your thoughts and contributions to this book—couldn't have done it without you.

To Cherie Rae, Greg Muller, Ian Patterson, Adam O'Brien, Tom Dalton and Sue Sestan—thanks for being my beta readers. Your suggestions and contributions have made this what it is!

To Carolyn Jackson, my editor—great teamwork. You have done so much by way of challenging, questioning and guiding!

To Scott and the publishing team at Grammar Factory—thanks for all the guidance and support. You made it so easy.

Finally, to all the good humans working to solve our social problems, this work is built on your efforts every day. It is about you and for you—THANK YOU!!!

ABOUT THE AUTHOR

GEORGE LIACOS has over twenty-seven years of hands-on experience working on strategy with and for the social and for-purpose sectors. He is the founder of Spark Strategy—one of the first and leading social sector strategic and impact advisory firms. Spark Strategy is a BCorp and operates around the world from its home bases in Melbourne and Sydney, Australia.

Spark Strategy (and its predecessor brand Projexion) has more than 600 case studies of strategy work done with the social and for-purpose sectors, and shares its sector capability building work through its many whitepapers, blogs, 'future of...' papers, Spark TV and other channels—all as part of its desire to help build capability in the for-purpose sector.

George and his business partner and close friend, Ian Patterson, are co-owners of the technology advisory and services business HumanIT, which also focuses on the for-purpose sector. Again, this is a business purpose built for social impact. George's businesses publish an annual impact report, which demonstrates the millions of dollars' worth of impact and support they deliver to the social sector. George has an MBA from The University of Melbourne and a Bachelor of Economics from the University of Sydney, and is a graduate of the Institute of Company Directors in both its Company Directors' and Chairman's courses.

George is also a sought-after public speaker, and talks to social sector, government and corporate audiences as an expert on strategy and purpose, with an emphasis on mental and physical health trends and impacts.

Usually George sits on a handful of Boards, but at the time of writing he has stepped back from his various Board and Chair roles in the sector to make space for this book and the supporting materials.

Let's connect

At Spark Strategy, we believe there's something extraordinary that happens when an idea gets the opportunity to flourish, to find its feet. We work to unleash their potential and transform organisations and the societies in which they live.

To book George as a speaker at your next event, as a media or podcast guest, or to discuss how Spark Strategy can help you and your team build your strategic thinking muscles, please contact us at info@sparkstrategy.com.au.

To connect on social media, please add Spark Strategy on your favourite social platforms:

LinkedIn   @sparkstrategy

YouTube   @sparkstrategy

Instagram   @sparkstrategyAU

X   @sparkstrategyAU

Facebook   @sparkstrategyAU

And be sure to visit www.sparkstrategy.com.au